# ACHIEVEMENT TEAMS

Many ASCD members received this book
as a member benefit upon its initial release.
Learn more at **www.ascd.org/memberbooks**.

• • • • •

# ACHIEVEMENT TEAMS

## How a Better Approach to PLCs Can Improve Student Outcomes and Teacher Efficacy

*Foreword by John Hattie*

**Steve Ventura**          **Michelle Ventura**

Arlington, Virginia USA

2800 Shirlington Road, Suite 1001 • Arlington, VA 22206 USA
Phone: 800-933-2723 or 703-578-9600 • Fax: 703-575-5400
Website: www.ascd.org • Email: member@ascd.org
Author guidelines: www.ascd.org/write

Penny Reinart, *Chief Impact Officer*; Genny Ostertag, *Managing Director, Book Acquisitions & Editing*; Allison Scott, *Senior Acquisitions Editor*; Julie Houtz, *Director, Book Editing*; Miriam Calderone, *Editor*; Thomas Lytle, *Creative Director*; Donald Ely, *Art Director*; Mary Duran and Derrick Douglas, *Graphic Designers*; Valerie Younkin, *Senior Production Designer*; Kelly Marshall, *Production Manager*; Shajuan Martin, *E-Publishing Specialist*

Figures i.1, i.3, 1.4, 1.6, 2.1, 2.4, 2.5, 2.9, 2.10, 5.2, 5.4, 5.5, 5.7, 6.2, 6.5, 7.2, 9.1, 9.2, 9.3, and 9.4 are copyright Steve Ventura. All are printed in this book with permission.

All web links in this book are correct as of the publication date below but may have become inactive or otherwise modified since that time. If you notice a deactivated or changed link, please email books@ascd.org with the words "Link Update" in the subject line. In your message, please specify the web link, the book title, and the page number on which the link appears.

PAPERBACK ISBN: 978-1-4166-3119-4     ASCD product #122034
PDF E-BOOK ISBN: 978-1-4166-3120-0; see Books in Print for other formats.
Quantity discounts are available: email programteam@ascd.org or call 800-933-2723, ext. 5773, or 703-575-5773. For desk copies, go to www.ascd.org/deskcopy.

ASCD Member Book No. FY22-7 (May 2022 P). ASCD Member Books mail to Premium (P), Select (S), and Institutional Plus (I+) members on this schedule: Jan, PSI+; Feb, P; Apr, PSI+; May, P; Jul, PSI+; Aug, P; Sep, PSI+; Nov, PSI+; Dec, P. For current details on membership, see www.ascd.org/membership.

**Library of Congress Cataloging-in-Publication Data**
Names: Ventura, Steve, author. | Ventura, Michelle, author.
Title: Achievement teams : how a better approach to PLCs can improve student outcomes and teacher efficacy / Steve Ventura and Michelle Ventura.
Description: Arlington, VA : ASCD, [2022] | Includes bibliographical references and index.
Identifiers: LCCN 2021056310 (print) | LCCN 2021056311 (ebook) | ISBN 9781416631194 (Paperback) | ISBN 9781416631200 (PDF)
Subjects: LCSH: Teaching teams. | Team learning approach in education. | Professional learning communities.
Classification: LCC LB1029.T4 V46 2022 (print) | LCC LB1029.T4 (ebook) | DDC 371.14/8—dc23/eng/20220209
LC record available at https://lccn.loc.gov/2021056310
LC ebook record available at https://lccn.loc.gov/2021056311

31  30  29  28  27  26  25  24  23  22          1  2  3  4  5  6  7  8  9  10  11  12

# ACHIEVEMENT TEAMS

How a Better Approach to PLCs Can Improve
Student Outcomes and Teacher Efficacy

# Foreword: Achievement Teams, the Key to Effective Collaboration

I am driven by the incredible number of successful schools I have visited and the many expert leaders and teachers I have been fortunate to meet as I travel the world. My mission is to change the focus of our current debates about schools, from finding fault and dreaming up fixes to finding success and upscaling it. This book focuses on upscaling success, not one teacher at a time but collectively, and makes it clear that it's rare to find a great school without a great leader who has a mission to improve the learning of every student and adult within it.

It took me many years of academic research on the concept of excellence and expertise to understand how this manifested itself in schools, a task made more difficult by a general tendency to blame the kids, the curriculum, the lack of resources and money, the structure of schools, and the parents for a school's less-than-optimal results. But in truth, what counts is the evaluative thinking of educators—the moment-by-moment decisions they make in the classroom; the decisions leaders make about how to use time, priorities, and resources; and the evaluations everyone makes about their effect on students and on students' magnitude of growth. This is all the more powerful if educators do this collectively. For this to occur in schools, we need evidence of educators' impact, and this is where Achievement Teams come in, early and often.

This book is based on a deep understanding of my work, and Steve Ventura has been a partner in delivery for many years. The Venturas understand that evidence leads to probabilities, not certainties. They know that a high-impact intervention is a probability, and that if it's poorly implemented, it will not yield high-impact results. The fundamental claim is that "$x$ is formative assessment and evaluation, $y$ is collective efficacy and collaboration, and $z$ is high-quality instructional strategies with higher levels of student achievement"—and that these elements are likely to lead to better outcomes for students. There are no fixed answers to the weights or proportions of $x$, $y$, and $z$ because these depend on the situation, the desired outcomes, the student, and so many other factors. The art is to dig deeply, be open to surprises, and always check for biases and misinterpretations.

The Venturas also clearly appreciate that collaboration, professional learning communities (PLCs), assessments, and evaluation must—note, *must*—focus on the impact that educators are having on students, and this entails a robust discussion about what the term *impact* means to each teacher and how transparent these notions and expectations are to the students. Too often, professional learning communities and collective efficacy are about peripheral and even unrelated topics. When he initially introduced PLCs, Rick DuFour was clear that they should relentlessly focus on fostering learning for all students, building a collaborative culture and collective effort to support student and adult learning, and continually improving practice (DuFour & Fullan, 2013). Too often, we wrongly consider just any group of educators meeting together a PLC. We cannot afford this same mistake to occur regarding the notion of collective efficacy or Achievement Teams. Achievement Teams are, at their core, about impact.

Thus, the three focuses of this book: what matters most; clarity; and—a word that can cause shivers—accountability. The first pertains to what the collective means by *impact*; the second to being clear about the criteria for success in a series of lessons (particularly in the minds of students); and the third to our responsibility in terms of the consequences of our thinking and actions on the learning lives of students. I don't mean accountability in the sense of the top-down standardized tests regime that has brought testing a bad name, but accountability in terms of investigating the effect we're having on students, learning to stop what we're doing if there isn't sufficient impact for all students, and upscaling and smelling the roses from the effect of our expertise when there is.

We have had *data teams, impact coaches,* and so many other "nicer" terms to ensure accountability, so here comes the next one: *Achievement Teams*. Understanding the effect we're having on students entails using evidence from test scores, assignments, observations of students working and their work, and listening to students talk about their learning. This triangulation of information is a core function of Achievement Teams; it ensures that we educators make defensible and appropriate action-leading interpretations and decisions based on this evidence. The Venturas call this process *evidence, inference,* and *impact*.

They are clear on this point. This is not only about whether students master the facts and gain the subject-matter vocabulary, but also about whether they acquire a depth of complexity in their understanding and thinking. The Venturas use Webb's Depth of Knowledge (Webb, 1997) to anchor this distinction (I use the SOLO Taxonomy of John Biggs and Kevin Collis [1982]). The crucial point is that we need both the surface and the depth, the knowing *that* and the knowing *how*. We need to ensure that our decisions take both into account, depending on our success criteria, the timing of the instruction, and the differentiated nature of the teaching.

I have often written that I'm not a fan of the terms *formative assessment* and *summative assessment*. They place too much emphasis on assessment and not enough on the formative and summative interpretations that occur during and at the end of a series of lessons. Bob Stake, Professor Emeritus of Education, summed it up like this: "When the cook tastes the soup, it's formative; when the guests taste the soup, it's summative." Both are important, both need to be reliable; it's a matter of *when* we make the interpretations. I prefer the terms *formative evaluation* and *summative evaluation* to emphasize that what matter most are the decisions educators make during or at the end of instruction, not the tests.

Many rich examples throughout the book illustrate this crucial distinction, and I particularly commend the message that *assessment information is feedback information to teachers about their impact*. If you think this way, it also leads to creating more informative assessments. If, after an assessment, you don't learn how to improve your teaching for all your students, the tests are probably wasting not only your time but your students' time as well. This book outlines many strategies for discussing what you learned from assessments with colleagues, from instructional rounds to coaching to microteaching to Achievement Teams.

Let me be clear: creating collaborative teams in schools is difficult. Many great teachers became great because they "did it themselves," but this doesn't lead to upscaling their success. Moreover, newer teachers don't want to enter or stay in a profession that is not collaborative. The problem is, schools and staff rooms are not dominated by discussions about the impact of teaching but, rather, about curriculum, students, assessments, and kicking footballs. Also, we often don't discuss impact on the grounds that we all teach differently, that we all "own" our own students—and how dare you question my success. This is where great leaders come in—their greatest power in a school is that they can mandate the focus of the narrative—and that narrative needs to be about the impact the adults are having on the students. It needs to remind every teacher that they came into this profession with one major motive: to have a positive effect on students' lives.

Research abounds concerning the key components of what leaders need to do. We need to develop three skills among teachers: the skill of contributing to groups; the skill of building one's confidence to contribute; and, the hardest, the skill of building the belief that the group can come up with better answers than each teacher alone. Without these attributes, we get contrived collegiality and dysfunctional groups, and we waste a lot of time. But stop! Look at the powerful effects when collective efficacy about impact works. It increases the rate of learning by a factor of three to four. When leaders develop collective efficacy and work in Achievement Teams, it's well worth it.

Leaders need to create safe and high-trust environments where difficult, open-to-learn conversations can take place without fear of shame or blame, where it's OK to talk about what's not working as well as about what's working well, where we reveal our beliefs about expectations and what a year's growth for a year's input looks like, where we collectively interpret data and give and receive feedback, and where everyone in the school sees the leader as the chief evaluator who leads all to become evaluators of their impact.

So start reading—and enjoy!

—Professor John Hattie, University of Melbourne

# Acknowledgments

Discussions about increasing school collaboration can be challenging. Amid myriad other school initiatives, some shudder at the thought of another collaborative protocol. Fortunately, there is an abundance of evidence that points to the positive effects of teacher collaboration—mainly, that it can improve the quality of teaching and its effect on student achievement. Based on these findings, we committed to writing a book that could help readers embark on a journey of discovery, focus, and self-reflection. We learned much about organizing thoughts and ideas with one main goal: creating a book that is compelling, engaging, and applicable.

There are many people to thank for helping us see our vision to completion. First, we thank Laura Besser, a colleague and friend, who supported the initial stages of development. When we first approached Laura, our idea was to create a training manual to accompany our professional development sessions. Once Laura guided us through this process, we enthusiastically began writing. However, within a month of starting this project, we realized the content we were producing was much more than a manual, and thus this project was born. Laura supported us throughout this endeavor, enabling us to produce our initial draft manuscript. She kept us focused and provided expert advice. We are indebted to her patience, feedback, and guidance. She truly is a consistent role model and motivator.

At Laura's suggestion, we invited Katie Stoddard to work with us as we continued to refine our manuscript. Katie became our content editor, providing timely feedback as we navigated through various chapters of information. Her keen eye and organizational skills provided us with valuable insight. Through countless hours of discussion, writing, editing, and revision, we deepened the content and sharpened the clarity of the manuscript, creating an end product that was not only informational, but broadly applicable as well. Like Laura, Katie brought with her a rich and experienced publishing background to help us realize our goal. She understood our desire to make schools a better place for colleagues, the people on the faculty and staff, as well as the greater community. We'd also like to thank our video editor, Mark Wieser of www.treehouseDV.com, for allowing us to capture the essence of Achievement Teams through video.

We feel honored to have forged personal relationships with major thought leaders from around the globe, including Professor John Hattie, whose research inspired much of this book's foundation. Steve was fortunate enough to partner with John for years, delivering Visible Learning professional development sessions. We are thrilled that John, himself a best-selling author and an award-winning researcher, wrote our foreword, capturing the essence of our book. His sincere contribution makes us beam with pride.

Dr. Douglas Reeves has had a major impact on us as well. Years ago, we traveled with Doug to Zambia, providing professional development to lecturers and professors from nine teacher colleges. Steve started his professional development career under Doug's mentorship. Doug is an expert on instructional leadership, and we refer to his research as we provide guidance to school leaders who want to thrive in their positions as learning leaders.

Jim Knight inspired us to research deeply and well with regard to applying practical strategies that advance instructional design while promoting great teaching and learning. Jim provides the perfect balance between research and application, and we refer to his findings to support instructional strategy implementation.

We would also like to thank ASCD, an exceptional organization for this partnership. We are delighted ASCD chose to publish this book, as the organization is a leading force in education. Our first encounter with the ASCD team was with Allison Scott, our Senior Acquisitions Editor. Her ability to grasp how this book is to be used and the information we included gave her the ability to provide us with complete clarity on how to craft a more refined product. She motivated us to complete everything within the specified dates and to make this the best book that it could be. We humbly thank Allison for her expertise and feedback.

As we neared the end of this project, we had the pleasure of working with Miriam Calderone, our ASCD editor. It was exciting to see how Miriam constructed the final edits, bringing everything together after months of smaller focus areas. Her contributions made us appreciate her talent and wisdom, and her friendly, warm communication provided us with the perfect balance between ideas and implementation. Miriam was also open, direct, efficient, and responsive to all of our questions, and we are thankful for our partnership.

Finally, we offer sincere gratitude to the countless number of educators who have invested in the Achievement Teams protocol. Thank you for the work you do and your commitment to collaboration that impacts teaching and learning every single day.

# How do I use a QR code?

**Step 1**

Open the camera on
your device.

**Step 2**

Point the camera at the
code. The camera will
automatically scan the code.

**Step 3**

A notification with a
link will appear on
screen. Tap the link.

**Step 4**

Success!

# Introduction:
# Welcome to Achievement Teams

*Happiness is not the belief that we don't need to change;*
*it's the realization that we can.*

—Shawn Achor

Education is one of the most personally and professionally rewarding career paths that one can choose, and we thank you for taking this illuminating journey with Achievement Teams. Teaching requires educators to possess a growth mindset—a belief that all kids can learn—as well as a desire to help students reach their dreams and aspirations and become lifelong learners. The education imperative is simple: we need to foster deep collaboration, encourage responsible autonomy, and create professionals who enthusiastically believe they can make a difference in the lives of all students.

Traveling across the United States as we help educators implement Achievement Teams has made us realize that education is not for the passive or for the person who prefers to work in a silo. With Achievement Teams, teachers use a process to make working together more productive. It's about having real conversations that have a beneficial effect on students. This process is a systematic treasure hunt for best practices using real data on your students, making collaboration more efficient, rigorous, and satisfying.

In an effort to establish the foundational layers of a school's academic dashboard, Achievement Teams turn research into common sense, into actionable steps that truly promote collective teacher efficacy.

Three Truths About School Improvement

School improvement is not easy work, and both leaders and teachers need to be dedicated to the mission to make real, lasting change. After decades of working both within schools and closely with leadership teams, we have discovered three truths about school improvement:

**1. A program will never have as much impact as your practice.** Anytime schools feel pressure to dramatically improve student outcomes, a common solution is to purchase additional resources or adopt more programs. Although this strategy may have some positive effects, the results never seem to match the investment. And if this were a viable solution, then why do so many schools continue to add on additional programs each year, even when a multitude of initiatives are currently in place? If this scenario sounds familiar, you're not alone. If your school or students are struggling, your first solution should not be to purchase another program.

However, teachers *can* increase their effectiveness by considering the power of contemporary, research-based instructional strategies. Effective instruction is much more likely than programs to improve the efficacy of both teachers and students. Achievement Teams are designed to increase the collective ability of teachers and leaders. Effective teachers make a far greater difference in learning than programs do, and although programs can add value to instruction, teaching is the significant variable. That's why leaders need to promote collaborative efforts, sustain those efforts, and allow for context-specific conversations.

**2. Instructional leaders don't "sponsor" learning for others. They *participate* in learning with others.** The best leaders are great teachers; it's that simple. Effective leaders maintain a learning environment based on quality teaching, student engagement, and evaluation of instructional impact, and they create positive home-school relationships. When leaders possess the knowledge, skills, and principles associated with high-yield leadership behaviors, they can have a positive effect on students and teachers.

From observing successful schools, especially our client schools, we have learned that Achievement Teams function better when they have leaders who commit to deep implementation of those practices that have the most significant effect. They monitor collaboration time, visit classrooms, and consistently participate in teacher learning; in this way, they become a valuable resource for teachers. Effective leaders are proactive, are supportive, and can identify those high-value tasks with a laser-like focus.

**3. Great schools move from islands of excellence to systematic impact with high levels of collective efficacy and commitment.** It would seem obvious that the more we focus on the things that matter most, the more we can improve. High-quality implementation also has a qualitative component. Teachers implement best when they are prepared, when they are clear, and when they teach with enthusiasm.

The most significant contribution to systematic impact is not more program implementation. *It's giving teachers more time to implement.* No body of research suggests that frantically covering everything will lead to better results. In fact, the research claims just the opposite, because "schools with higher levels of focus not only have higher levels of student achievement but are also better able to implement other essential leadership and teaching strategies" (Reeves, 2010).

Schools attempting to reform should commit to deeply implementing just two or three changes and finish those before launching other initiatives. This approach is more effective than superficial implementation of a wide variety of strategies because deep, consistent implementation will predictably narrow achievement gaps. When educational organizations determine the most important practices and commit to sustaining those practices, costs will actually decrease because of better-informed resource allocation and a drastic reduction in student failures. At the same time, they will be implementing a culture of collective teacher efficacy.

Sadly, schools rarely consider these recommendations. As a result, we waste time, energy, and precious resources on "secret sauce" programs that schools can neither sustain nor adequately monitor. Our sincere hope is that this book helps readers create a sense of purpose and that it becomes a catalyst to forming positive, long-lasting habits that will make collaborative teams far more effective.

## An Overview of Collaborative Teams

Members of effective teams understand that their collective impact is what fuels quality collaboration—especially when the emphasis is on improved instruction. When collaborative protocols become a fundamental practice, teams will have a more significant effect on teaching, learning, and leadership. Ultimately, a commitment to collaborate means continuous improvement for all students. Strengthening collective efficacy in schools, or the shared belief that teachers can accomplish the goals they have set, is not just about creating more time to collaborate; the structure of collaboration time must be purposeful as well. If we expect teachers to engage in professional dialogue, then the conversation must be productive and robust.

As you start this journey with Achievement Teams, we invite you to clearly define what accountability means to you as an educator and to your school as a community of learners. Achievement Teams have an impact when there's a commitment to individual and collective accountability. When teams collaborate and agree on expectations, members are more likely to honor those commitments and work together to reach their goals. Achievement Teams create a culture that strengthens leadership, fosters positive relationships, and provides the tools to improve teaching and learning.

## Why Teams Fail

Many schools and districts have decided that professional learning communities (PLCs) are the best strategy for improving student achievement. However, these same organizations often experiment with a collaborative protocol and then abandon PLCs as soon as the next trendy initiative comes along. Even more problematic is the phrase *professional learning community* itself. In truth, the term has lost its meaning in many schools. In some instances, when two or more people have a conversation—about anything!—it's called a PLC. In the absence of protocols and disciplined collaboration, a PLC may be nothing more than a general staff meeting.

Typically, teacher teams are dysfunctional for a number of reasons. A primary one is that the process is hurried and rarely thought out (Venables, 2011). Well-intentioned principals or system-level leaders have bestowed the title of "data team" or "PLC" on teams of educators. The expectation is that the teams will jump into the work of PLCs—examining student work and short-cycle assessments, looking at data, and so on—with little or no focus. However, authentic teams are not something forced on educators or mandated to the staff in a school, despite the fact that many so-called PLCs have been designed exactly this way. Instead of issuing mandates, we should harness our collective efforts by creating a sustainable and realistic model of collective efficacy where teams don't need to be forced to meet, where they look at collaboration as a means to address professional goals that increase student achievement.

## What Are Achievement Teams?

Purposeful collaboration is the single best way to help educators and administrators move from "hyperdata analysis" to using assessment results that lead to better instructional decisions. What makes the Achievement Teams process distinctive is that we're not just looking at student scores, but rather at a combination of antecedents, student results, evidence statements, teaching strategies, and leadership support.

Achievement Teams are a collaborative protocol that focuses on appropriating new knowledge about teaching and learning rather than simply maintaining existing knowledge. Within Achievement Teams, educators look at student data to make decisions about instruction and teaching practices that need to shift to best meet student needs.

With Achievement Teams, participants follow protocols consistently while challenging current thinking and practice. Structure replaces loose guidelines. When those meeting protocols are embedded in school practice, teams will have a more significant effect on teaching, learning, and leadership. Ultimately, a commitment to collaborate means greater achievement for all students.

We are acutely aware of the research and writing around professional learning communities. If your school has already established collaboration time, then this book may represent a new shift in focus around team meetings. If your teams have no specific guidance or protocols, then you can follow our step-by-step process for empowering collaboration. Whatever level your school is at, this book will add value to any school or district wishing to increase its collaborative potential.

## The Achievement Teams Framework

The Achievement Teams framework (see Figure i.1, p. 7) is a conceptual structure that clarifies the purpose of meaningful collaboration. Here, we introduce three important factors that provide the foundation for an Achievement Teams cycle:

- **Evidence:** Achievement Teams focus on evidence from quality short-cycle assessments and use data to help determine high-leverage instructional strategies.
- **Inference:** Achievement Teams help teachers and leaders make accurate inferences about the levels of mastery that students have achieved with respect to a specific learning target.
- **Impact:** Achievement Teams focus only on those instructional strategies that have the potential to considerably accelerate student achievement.

**REFLECTION ACTIVITY**

Assessing Your Level of Collaboration

Assess your current level of collaboration using the Likert scale below.

1-----------2-----------3-----------4-----------5

1 = Nonpracticing; this has not yet been established.
2 = Initial stages; we are starting to take action.
3 = Progressing; there are small pockets of success.
4 = Partial implementation, but this could not be considered common practice.
5 = This is common practice in our school.

Explain why you gave yourself this rating. What has been established and is currently working? What are your biggest weaknesses in terms of collaboration?

## The Achievement Teams Four-Step Meeting Protocol

Achievement Teams involve a four-step meeting protocol with a continuous cycle. We will explain the four-step protocol and model it in detail in Chapters 5–8 of this book, but following is a brief overview:

**Step 1: Collect and chart the data.**

Achievement Teams focus on evidence from quality short-cycle assessments.

**Step 2: Set SMART goals.**

Creating goals for both students and teachers has a tremendous effect on academic outcomes.

**Step 3: Create baseline evidence statements.**

Summarizing collected data helps educators make inferences around students' mastery levels.

**Step 4: Select high-yield instructional strategies.**

Teachers select the strategies that will have the greatest effect on student achievement.

**FIGURE i.1**    The Achievement Teams Framework

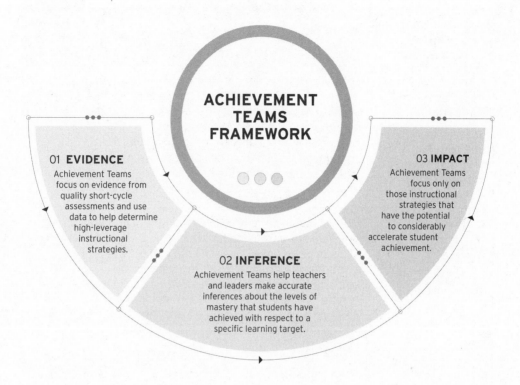

This protocol provides a structure for teachers to accurately reflect on teaching between pre- and post-assessments while simultaneously identifying areas of student need. Teachers then collaboratively decide on the best corrective instructional approach in response to those needs. When schools and school systems deemphasize individual practice and promote collective ability, they can create professional teams of educators who continuously reflect on and improve their practice.

## The Critical Components of Achievement Teams

Six of the high-impact findings from the Visible Learning research (Hattie, 2009) are major components of the Achievement Teams process, and we call those practices *critical components* because of their collective power in teaching and learning (see Figures i.2 and i.3). When these critical components work together, they lead to increased levels of collective teacher efficacy.

**FIGURE i.2**   The Critical Components: Visible Learning
Ratings and Achievement Team Alignment

| Achievement Teams Critical Components | Description | Achievement Teams Alignment |
|---|---|---|
| **1. Formative Assessment and Evaluation**<br><br>Visible Learning Rating: Likely to have a positive impact on student achievement | Formative assessment occurs in many schools and districts; however, the results of those assessments may not lead to elevated levels of student progress. This can only occur when teachers understand that formative assessment is designed to assist teachers in evaluating their instructional impact. | **Step 1.** Collect and chart the data. |
| **2. Goal Setting**<br><br>Visible Learning Rating: Potential to accelerate student achievement | Creating goals for both students and teachers has a tremendous effect on academic outcomes. Goals lead to better student self-assessment, self-evaluation, and self-monitoring of progress. When teachers regularly create and include challenging goals, they motivate students to exert effort in line with the difficulty of a task (Hattie, 2009). | **Step 2.** Set SMART goals. |
| **3. Feedback**<br><br>Visible Learning Rating: Potential to considerably accelerate student achievement | Providing accurate and timely feedback to both students and teachers can help promote a collaborative atmosphere conducive to specific student needs. When feedback is combined with effective instruction, it can be powerful in enhancing learning. Achievement Teams incorporate a feedback model that encourages the use of task, process, and self-regulation feedback based on assessment results. | **Step 1.** Collect and chart the data.<br><br>**Step 2.** Set SMART goals.<br><br>**Step 4.** Select high-yield instructional strategies. |
| **4. Response to Intervention (RTI)**<br><br>Visible Learning Rating: Potential to considerably accelerate student achievement | Achievement Teams and RTI work well together because RTI circumvents a "wait to fail" situation. Teachers provide timely assistance to students between a pre- and post-assessment cycle. In addition, teachers who possess high levels of collective efficacy refer fewer students to special education because they are able to respond to student needs within a general education setting. | **Step 3.** Create baseline evidence statements.<br><br>**Step 4.** Select high-yield instructional strategies. |

| Achievement Teams Critical Components | Description | Achievement Teams Alignment |
|---|---|---|
| **5. Teacher Clarity**<br><br>Visible Learning Rating: Potential to considerably accelerate student achievement | Teacher clarity is all about clearly communicating learning targets and success criteria. A major Achievement Teams prerequisite skill is the ability to create specific learning progressions based on an identified learning target. | **Step 3.** Create baseline evidence statements.<br><br>**Step 4.** Select high-yield instructional strategies. |
| **6. Collective Teacher Efficacy (CTE)**<br><br>Visible Learning Rating: Potential to considerably accelerate student achievement | CTE is the overall belief that teachers can have a greater influence on student achievement when they combine their collective efforts. The organization of the team, how they work together, and the strategies they choose to achieve academic goals contribute significantly to efficacious behavior. | **All Four Steps** |

**FIGURE i.3**   Six Critical Components

Why did we choose these six components? Because they help create a culture of evidence. In his Visible Learning research, John Hattie (2009) identified dozens of highly influential instructional practices. It's impossible to implement all of those practices. In fact, one of the most common misconceptions about Visible Learning implementation is that the top 10 practices will transform your school or district. That's not how we should use the findings. We should use them to help educators determine what works best with specific student needs.

The Achievement Teams protocol doesn't feature a "top 10" list; we did, however, select these six components because they consistently align with our collaborative protocol. They appear throughout the process, and we intentionally embedded them in specific Achievement Teams steps.

## The Research Behind Achievement Teams

Achievement Teams have their roots in the most extensive summary of educational research—John Hattie's *Visible Learning* (2009). The components of Achievement Teams intentionally align with the teacher and leadership profiles and influences that have the greatest effects on student achievement.

Hattie continues to update the research base to reflect the most current practices in education. Moreover, the Achievement Teams framework revises resources and processes to reflect the changing needs of educators. However, some timeless practices remain constant and have an immediate effect on student achievement:

- Holding high expectations for *all* students and adults
- Providing multiple opportunities for students to demonstrate proficiency
- Knowing the purpose of learning, the process of learning, and the learning goals
- Using specific feedback to close gaps in achievement
- Collaborating to improve collective impact and effective instruction

Throughout this book, we refer to the Visible Learning research because it's embedded in Achievement Teams. That research showed that the average effect size was 0.4, meaning that students typically accomplish a year's worth of growth during a single year of schooling. Educators were quick to point out that many students need more than one year's worth of growth in one instructional year, and herein lies the value of this research: the practices that we have incorporated into Achievement Teams can considerably accelerate student achievement. That said, we have avoided using specific effect sizes because as Hattie continues to identify what matters most, the effects are likely to change.

In a recent white paper, Hattie and Hamilton (2020) explain, "There are no known universal laws of learning (yet). At best, the findings from Visible Learning can be considered 'probability claims': *if you implement* x *under* y *conditions, there is a high probability you will have* z *effect"* (p. 7).

Achievement Teams contain a "probability claim": In this case, the *x* is formative assessment and evaluation, the *y* is collective efficacy and collaboration, and the *z* is high-quality instructional strategies with higher levels of student achievement. Achievement Teams create conditions where the probability of yielding high effects is present throughout the entire process.

## Mindframes and Achievement Teams

In *10 Mindframes for Visible Learning*, Hattie and Zierer (2018) describe mindframes that are likely to have a considerable effect on student learning. Mindframes are ways of thinking that predicate how we act as educators. Achievement Team members base their collaborative conversations around two crucial mindframes:

- My fundamental task is to evaluate the effect of my teaching on students' learning and achievement.
- All assessments, including formative assessments, are a reflection more of my effort than of my students' effort. (Hattie & Zierer, 2018)

Concerning this second mindframe, Hattie and Zierer are pointing out that the adults have the ability to evaluate and interpret assessment results—and then make instructional adjustments.

Hattie and Zierer write that educational expertise is "a product of exchange and cooperation" among teachers. In an Achievement Teams meeting, teachers develop collective intelligence, solve complex problems about student learning, and develop a rigorous instructional plan. Teams are systematic about their approach to adult learning, and, as a result, teaching can accelerate learning for all students continuously. Achievement Teams build the educational expertise needed to close achievement gaps for students.

## Collective Efficacy and the Success of Collaborative Teams

In his extensive research, John Hattie calls out collective teacher efficacy as a top influence on student achievement. According to psychologist Albert Bandura (1997), *collective efficacy* refers to a "group's shared belief in its conjoint capabilities to organize and execute the courses of action required to produce given levels of attainment" (p. 477).

Bandura (1986) and Goddard, Hoy, and Hoy (2000) have identified four sources of efficacy:

1. Master experiences
2. Vicarious experiences
3. Social and verbal persuasion
4. Positive emotional and physiological states

**Master experiences** are performance accomplishments and have the greatest influence on shaping and building one's self-efficacy (Bandura, 1986). Because successful experiences increase expectations for the achievement of goals, self-efficacy improves. For example, when a teacher demonstrates mastery in a specific instructional strategy and the application of that strategy has a positive effect on student learning, the teacher experiences a self-belief in that area. Typically, master experiences are the result of determination and persistence.

**Vicarious experiences** occur as a result of observing colleagues, especially those who successfully perform in challenging conditions (Bandura, 1986). When people see others successfully attaining their goals through determination and persistence, it motivates them to increase their own belief in demonstrating mastery.

**Social and verbal persuasion** occurs when teachers and leaders are led by suggestion into believing they can successfully cope with challenging situations (Bandura, 1986). Bandura (1986, 2000) found that schools with high levels of social and verbal persuasion had a culture of openness, cooperation, and trust when facing challenges and trying to improve student learning.

**Positive emotional and physiological states** are the final sources of collective efficacy. When teachers face what seems like an overwhelming challenge, a safe environment permits risk taking and alleviates anxiety. Teams can build collective efficacy by focusing efforts on the emotional tone and environment of the school.

A crucial factor leading to successful collaboration is the belief that what the group is doing can make a difference and that their work is worth the time and effort. The organization of the team, how team members work together, and the strategies they choose to achieve academic goals contribute significantly to efficacious behavior. Successful collaboration takes place in team meetings, when professional development is extended into the classroom, and during coaching sessions.

What teachers need is time—time to go deeper with fewer initiatives and focus on practices that have the most potential to have an effect on student learning. Inspired and passionate teachers who believe they can positively affect their students' educational growth are strongly correlated to increased student achievement. With the formation of Achievement Teams and the purposeful commitment to working collectively, teachers will have more influence on student learning than any program ever will.

 **The Many Benefits of Collective Efficacy**

The philosophy behind using collaboration as a form of improving teaching and leadership is simple: teachers can have a greater influence on student achievement when they combine their collective efforts. In addition to the beneficial effects on student achievement, schools and districts can enjoy many other important benefits from maintaining high levels of focused collaboration.

In 2006, RAND researcher Cassandra Guarino and associates analyzed federal Schools and Staffing Surveys (Guarino, Santibañez, & Daley, 2006). The study uncovered lower turnover rates among teachers who met regularly to share, refine, and assess the effects of lessons and strategies that focused on increasing the number of students learning at higher levels. After surveying 2,000 current and former teachers in California, researcher Ken Futernick (2007) concluded that when teachers believed in their efficacy, were involved in decision making, and established strong collegial relationships, they felt greater personal satisfaction.

## Why Achievement Teams Work

To clarify, the Achievement Teams process is not a program; it's a framework that any school or district can replicate. It's built on collaborative philosophies and processes that elevate collective efficacy. A program will typically lose sustainability with a change in faculty or leadership, but sound professional practice, like that which we see in Achievement Teams, never goes out of style. With determination, focus, and a belief that effective collaboration is worth doing, Achievement Teams can become the culture of your school or district and will ultimately lead to improved student learning.

**REFLECTION ACTIVITY**

Collaboration and Teacher Efficacy

You may be a current member of an Achievement Team or another collaborative protocol, or you may be new to the process altogether. What are the implications of increasing collective teacher efficacy as a result of deeper levels of collaboration?

## How to Use This Book

Our goal in writing this book is twofold: to support you as you meet in Achievement Teams and as you continue on your PLC journey. The book begins with our definition of Achievement Teams and how they can support teacher collaboration and learning. In the early chapters, we provide guidance on how to select teams and how teams best function. We also review some general practices that support the process, such as assessment types, learning progressions, success criteria, and more. In later chapters, we explore all four steps of Achievement Teams, referencing videos and other resources throughout. We end the book with additional details and strategies to help you and your team get started.

### Reflection Activities

Throughout the book, we have included reflection activities; we indicate these with a reflection activity icon. These exercises are meant to guide your learning and can be completed by an individual or as a group. Some teams use the reflection activities during meetings to guide discussion and collaboration.

### Leadership Lens

We also have included content that is geared toward school and district leaders who will support the implementation of Achievement Teams; we indicate this content with the "Leadership Lens" icon seen here. Although all educators can benefit from these insights, they were designed to provide instructional leaders with the tools and content they need to further collaboration within their schools and districts.

### Resources Website and QR Codes

We have included numerous resources and templates throughout this book on our website at www.steveventura.com/achievement-teams. In addition, we have embedded QR codes such as the one shown here throughout the book to link to videos and other resources that dig deeper into Achievement Teams and illustrate best practices for implementing the structure.

## Key Takeaways

- The Achievement Teams framework is a collaborative protocol in which teams work collectively to form common goals designed to increase student learning.
- The components of Achievement Teams are based on six findings from John Hattie's Visible Learning research that have the greatest effect on student achievement.
- Achievement Teams use evidence, inference, and impact to elevate collective efficacy and collaboration.

# 1

# Setting Up the
# Achievement Team

*Isolation is the enemy of learning.*

—National Association of Elementary School Principals

In recent years, teacher collaboration has deepened and now has a much broader influence on educational outcomes. Many schools and districts now focus on improving and expanding teacher impact, encouraging teachers to share their strategies as they accelerate student achievement. Achievement Teams do just that.

With Achievement Teams, members are responsible for a number of tasks. The most important among them are evaluating their instructional impact and identifying gaps in learning. Once a team has identified those gaps, members can begin to address them.

## How Do We Create Teams?

Forming Achievement Teams is a joint responsibility of building leadership and team participants, although teams often form organically. The size of the teams and the number of teams at a single site are based on school size, faculty size, and other factors. An ideal team size would be three to six teachers, with at least two and generally no more than seven members to a team.

Based on our personal observation, there are three common models of team formation:

- Horizontal teams
- Vertical teams
- Specialist and elective teams

## Horizontal Teams

Forming horizontal teams is probably the most common approach to bringing teachers together because these teams typically consist of teachers from the same grade level and content area (see Figure 1.1). Horizontal teams develop and administer common formative assessments and share the same goals and purpose. For example, after reviewing assessment results and other grade-level indicators, horizontal teams may consider revising their focus based on the evidence they have collected. This focus can target a subject area, an identified student population, or even micro-trend data, like data related to question rigor (easy, medium, or hard).

**FIGURE 1.1**   Horizontal Algebra I Achievement Team

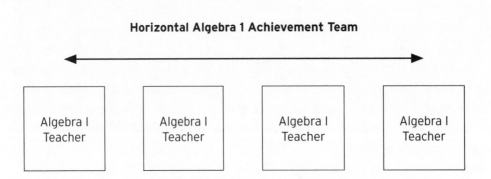

## Vertical Teams

Vertical teams (see Figure 1.2) can be just as effective as horizontal teams. In our experience, having worked in the roles of teacher, principal, and district superintendent, some schools simply do not have enough grade-level teachers to form a horizontal team. However, this need not be a cause for alarm, because many opportunities and configurations support vertical teaming.

For example, small or rural schools use vertically aligned teams to maximize collaboration while creating learning opportunities or grade-level progressions. Members of a vertical team may not be able to administer a common formative assessment, but they can use formative assessments specific to their content area.

Vertical teams can focus on vertically aligned content areas, like math and English language arts (ELA). Many curriculum guides are written in a manner that makes this possible. For example, a vertical ELA team might consist of one 4th grade teacher, one 5th grade teacher, and one 6th grade teacher. Even though team members cannot administer the same assessment, they can assess vertical skills, such as students' ability to compare and contrast, analyze text, and determine the central idea in a text. Such an assessment can provide tremendous insight into how students perform as they matriculate from one grade level to the next.

Vertical team members can

- Share their individual assessment results.
- Share how they teach a lesson.
- Share student work samples.

**FIGURE 1.2**   Vertical ELA Achievement Team

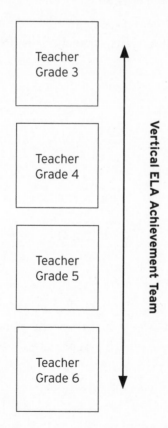

Schools can design vertical teams in other ways. Some schools may have leadership teams made up of a teacher representative from each horizontal or vertical

Achievement Team. In this situation, the teacher representatives meet to discuss common goals, strengths, and weaknesses trending across grade-level and curricular areas. This vertical team can develop a schoolwide focus on strengthening effective teaching strategies, creating a shared vocabulary, and providing support structures for students to successfully move from one grade level to the next. Even more compelling are vertical teams' opportunities to cross-reference horizontal work and continue to recognize and close gaps in schoolwide learning. For example, a P.E. teacher in a vertical team who is focusing on nonfiction writing may cross-reference scoring guides and success criteria from grade-level horizontal teams and use them to instill commonalities. This supports all educators working toward a schoolwide goal and gives them a common language and focus.

## Specialist and Elective Teams

These teams consist of teachers who may have a single prep or content area. Following are some examples of areas that specialist teams may pull from:

- Foreign language
- Choir
- Physical education
- Music and band
- Art
- Coding and technology
- Health
- Life skills
- Religion
- Auto mechanics
- Business accounting

Specialist teams represent the most diverse teaming. However, a common thread runs through them. Many of these team members will have taught the same students; they also have multiple opportunities to collaborate around common targets. Elective teachers who collaborate typically base that collaboration on target areas stressed by core teaching classrooms.

For example, in many of our clients' schools, elective teachers agree that writing is essential in specialist disciplines. Beyond promoting strong literacy, writing as an instructional strategy has led to increased levels of student success in just about all areas of the curriculum. If a specialist team were to address this topic, teachers in the various electives would ask their students to respond to different writing prompts, but they all would use the same scoring guide or rubric to assess the writing.

For example, physical education teachers might ask students to write about this volleyball prompt:

> *If you could add two rules to volleyball, what would they be and why? Include two to three reasons to support your thinking.*

There is a common pushback from teachers about assigning writing in elective classes: "We don't teach writing." The fact is, you don't need to be a writing teacher to know if students can summarize a text or locate the main idea. And ferreting out this information can be exceptionally helpful, to both the student and the teacher.

## What About Time?

Clients often ask us how long an Achievement Team meeting should last. The answer is, it depends. Schools and districts have dedicated a different number of collaboration minutes depending on their schedules. When teachers have a set time to meet, it's best not to saddle that time with a long agenda or other administrative duties. In one cycle, typically over the course of one month, Achievement Teams will meet twice; they'll meet first for the pre-assessment review and then, approximately two to three weeks later, for the post-assessment review.

The pre-assessment meeting should focus on increasing collaboration around the following four-step Achievement Teams protocol to improve teaching strategies and student achievement:

**Step 1.** Collect and chart the data.
**Step 2.** Set SMART goals.
**Step 3.** Create baseline evidence statements.
**Step 4.** Select high-yield instructional strategies.

Generally, the first two steps don't require as much time as the last two because they're preparing for the deeper discussions that occur later on. Often, teams will have already entered their assessment results into a collection form we provide (Step 1). This form uses a simple algorithm to suggest a SMART goal between the pre- and post-assessment in the specific area the teachers are targeting (Step 2). The first two steps should drive the subsequent conversation around what is and isn't working for students (Step 3) and allow plenty of time to determine which instructional strategies teachers will implement (Step 4). A good rule of thumb is the 20/80 principle: Steps 1 and 2 should take about 20 percent of the time, and Steps 3 and 4 should take about 80 percent of the time.

Figure 1.3 shows recommended timing suggestions for all four steps in meetings that last from 45 to 90 minutes. Teams should find the time allotments that work best for them depending on need.

The post-assessment meeting is a synthesis of the whole process and provides an opportunity for educators to determine whether they attained their goals. During this session, team members assess their impact as teachers and leave with summative statements about what worked in that cycle, how many students are still struggling, and whether they need to provide additional buffer instruction. A post-assessment meeting does not require as much time as a pre-assessment meeting.

**FIGURE 1.3**  Sample Achievement Teams Time Allotment

| Total Time | Steps 1 and 2 | Minutes | Steps 3 and 4 | Minutes |
|---|---|---|---|---|
| **45 minutes** | 20% of the meeting | **9** | 80% of the meeting | **36** |
| **60 minutes** | 20% of the meeting | **12** | 80% of the meeting | **48** |
| **75 minutes** | 20% of the meeting | **15** | 80% of the meeting | **60** |
| **90 minutes** | 20% of the meeting | **18** | 80% of the meeting | **72** |

## What About Roles?

To be successful in this work, teachers on an Achievement Team must believe they have the power to design engaging lessons and implement highly effective instructional strategies that will lead to student success. Everyone on the team should feel that they have a voice and can make a difference in their students' lives. According to Jim Knight (2019), team members become responsibly accountable "to students, parents, other stakeholders, and the profession of teaching. Responsible accountability entails a genuine individual commitment to learning and growth" (para. 14).

For teams to work smoothly, active member participation is a must. In addition, a number of roles should be assigned, such as facilitator, data recorder, timekeeper, and accuracy monitor. Instructional leaders will want to identify the facilitator as someone who can keep members engaged and focused. We also recommend that the person in this role has a strong understanding of instruction and assessment. Other roles can be determined within the rest of the team. Figure 1.4 lists the various roles and their responsibilities.

**FIGURE 1.4**   Achievement Team Roles

**Facilitator**
- ☑ Reviews norms and sets the focus
- ☑ Keeps the group on task
- ☑ Encourages everyone to participate
- ☑ Helps set the agenda for the next meeting

**Data Recorder**
- ☑ Collects the data by an identified date
- ☑ Records ideas and input from the meeting
- ☑ Asks the group for feedback on accuracy
- ☑ Communicates and shares the final record to the group and administrators, as needed

**Timekeeper**
- ☑ Divides the time for tasks
- ☑ Keeps the group moving through the four-step protocol based on the 20/80 rule
- ☑ Gives periodic signals as to how the time allotment is progressing

**Accuracy Monitor**
- ☑ Verifies instructional strategies
- ☑ Monitors consistent implementation
- ☑ Fact-checks resources

**Active Participants**
- ☑ Collaborate with others using a growth mindset
- ☑ Come to meetings prepared and on time
- ☑ Seek and provide data and input
- ☑ Actively engage in discussion
- ☑ Monitor self-adherence to norms
- ☑ Stay focused on the agenda, purpose, and goals of the meeting

# A Monthly Pacing Guide

Achievement Teams work best when they take time to set up pre- and post-assessment cycles to monitor both student achievement and teacher impact. Figure 1.5 shows an Achievement Team cycle that takes place over a month, between the beginning and the end of an instructional unit.

**FIGURE 1.5**  Sample Pacing Calendar for Achievement Teams

| Monday | Tuesday | Wednesday | Thursday | Friday |
|---|---|---|---|---|
| **Start of Unit 1** | Instruction | Instruction | Instruction | Instruction |
| **Administer pre-assessment** | **Achievement Team pre-assessment meeting** | Instruction | Instruction | Instruction |
| Instruction | Instruction | Instruction | Instruction | Instruction |
| **Administer post-assessment** | **Achievement Team post-assessment meeting** | Buffer | Buffer | **End of Unit 1** |

In this sample cycle, the teachers will pre-teach content before administering the first assessment. After the pre-assessment, team members will analyze the results in conjunction with the Achievement Team four-step process. Teachers will then have eight days to prepare for the post-assessment. Once they administer the post-assessment, two buffer days are built into the cycle for remediation or acceleration of student learning.

## Three Accelerators of Success

Three "accelerators" help teams increase their overall effectiveness: focus, clarity, and accountability. They establish a vision of excellence that encourages teams to move forward by fostering personal ownership and transparency.

### Accelerator 1: Focus

Focus requires an honest assessment of where we are and then prioritizes where we need to be. When teams can identify a level of focused collaboration, with team members agreeing on what students should learn and what teachers should assess—most often, an important learning target or skill that teachers have noticed many students need development in—engagement levels increase and motivation and enthusiasm thrive.

In her book *Smart Tribes* (2013), Cristine Comaford explains that focus includes the ability to *prioritize* high-value activities and *manage* the low-value tasks that waste time. The psychological advantages of implementation increase when teachers and other stakeholders realize that to accomplish something significant, they will need to discontinue other tasks deemed insignificant or ineffective, such as worksheets, homework at the primary level, excessive surface-level instruction, and other regressive teaching practices that are not rigorous or engaging enough for students.

Focus is paramount as we approach those learning intentions and instructional strategies that we must address *now*. If you have ever observed or been a member of a highly functioning team, you probably know that focus acts as an energizer and is the driving force behind meaningful collaboration.

## Accelerator 2: Clarity

Changing systems of collaboration and assessment requires a considerable degree of clarity. In fact, PLCs and other collaborative protocols often fail because of a lack of clarification about the meaning, purpose, and expectations of the team. To provide clarity for team members, it's beneficial to create criteria for meeting protocols—specifically norms. Figure 1.6 lists some sample success criteria, or norms, that do just that.

As the figure shows, success criteria for meetings provide teams with explicit behaviors that will improve meeting conditions, thus providing opportunities for validation and new thinking.

**FIGURE 1.6**   Success Criteria for Effective Collaboration

In successful collaboration, team members
- Understand that assessment results reflect their instructional effort.
- Understand that their primary function is to evaluate the effect of their teaching.
- Bring resources to meetings, including assessment results and student work samples and evidence.
- Share master and vicarious experiences focused on improving instructional success.
- Create and review norms before meetings and adhere to the meeting time and purpose.
- Build relational trust so collaboration can occur under the most positive conditions, where mistakes are OK and learning from others is essential.

But such clarity is not always the case in schools. One of the most frustrating issues with initiative implementation is the lack of clarity from building or system-level leadership. In this chaotic environment, teams resort to lower-level teaching and learning, with an emphasis on confusion. When teachers and leaders don't outwardly state the purpose, function, and desired outcomes of each meeting, it leads to generalized, and often incorrect, assumptions about the goal. Teams lose momentum, struggle with collaboration, and never truly get to appreciate the results of their efforts. Moreover, the promise of appropriating new knowledge about teaching and learning never reaches full potential. In fact, bad PLCs are worse than no PLCs because they perpetuate bad pedagogy.

## Accelerator 3: Accountability

When we talk about accountability for Achievement Teams, we mean much more than just improving outcomes. Team accountability begins with recognizing individuals first and then creating a vibrant, energized, and passionate group of educators who understand the power of their collective impact. Without this accountability, it's much more difficult for teams to reach their desired goals.

Team members want to know what they're supposed to accomplish and what they're accountable for. Team accountability begins with the following foundational expectations:

**Teacher teams will**
- See the value in following collaborative protocols consistently.
- Monitor progress and look for opportunities to improve collaboration.
- Reflect on results and accomplishments.
- Celebrate success and acknowledge challenges.
- Recognize success and learn how to replicate it.
- Make instructional adjustments.
- Share progress and best practices with one another.

But it's not just up to team members. School leaders have a crucial role to play, too. They must provide encouragement and support, and they need to understand that the *degree* of implementation makes the greatest difference. In high-performing schools, the leadership is more directly involved in coordinating the curriculum across grade levels than in lower-performing schools (Heck, Marcoulides, & Lang, 1991). Moreover, teachers in higher-performing schools report that their leaders are actively involved in collegial discussion of instructional matters, including how instruction affects student achievement (Heck et al., 1991).

**REFLECTION ACTIVITY**

Effective Collaborative Teams

Have you ever been a member of a highly functioning team? What helped guide the team to reach its goals? Reflect on your experience and record the behaviors and actions that contributed to the team's success.

**Conditions Present When You Were
a Member of an Effective Team**

Now compare the conditions you and your colleagues recorded with the success criteria in Figure 1.6.

## "But We Don't Have Time to Meet!"

Although having a dedicated meeting time is always a best practice, some teams struggle to find time to meet on a regular basis. When this happens, we encourage teams to be creative. Here are some suggestions:

- Teams find a single professional learning day when they can spend a greater amount of time planning as a group.
- Teams break meetings into smaller sessions that occur more frequently, such as meeting 10 or 15 minutes every day.
- Teams accomplish meeting protocols on their own and collaborate through a community platform like Slack or Microsoft Teams to engage in conversations over the course of a week or another timeframe. This works best when teams keep consistent timelines and deadlines.

## Best Practices for Virtual Achievement Teams

Virtual teams are common practice. Teachers from multiple buildings might form a virtual team to save travel time to meetings, or it might just be easier to meet virtually for other reasons. Whatever the impetus, Achievement Teams can be successful from a distance when teams follow these guidelines. Team members should

- Commit to team roles, even from a distance.
- Create a shareable spreadsheet to collect data and make sure all team members can see and access the sheet.
- Have their cameras on so everyone sees one another and stays focused on the meeting time and goals.

## Key Takeaways

- Achievement Teams can take the form of horizontal teams, vertical teams, or specialized teams.
- Focus, clarity, and accountability drive the success of Achievement Teams.
- Setting success criteria for effective collaboration enables the team to create an environment grounded in collective efficacy.
- Finding and prioritizing time to meet virtually or in person will enable Achievement Teams to have the greatest impact.

# 2

# Teacher Clarity and Learning Progressions

*Clarity affords focus.*

—Thomas Leonard

Careful planning is crucial for the Achievement Teams process, and it's essential for high-impact teaching. In fact, thought leader Michael Absolum (2011) believes it's the precursor to instruction. This chapter is devoted to the work that occurs *before* Achievement Teams begin a teaching and learning cycle.

Learner-centered classrooms are filled with challenge, choice, voice, and opportunity for leadership. A learner-centered environment is grounded in research, uses replicable practices, allows for differentiation, and leads to higher levels of learning. Students and teachers in classrooms such as this share an essential component—clarity of the teaching and learning process.

## Defining Teacher Clarity

Frank Fendick (1990) described teacher clarity as an organizational and instructional strategy focused on creating explicit learning targets and success criteria. In other words, teachers state something clearly rather than providing unclear or implicit directions. The difference between these two variables, implicit and explicit, is quite significant. With a notable effect size, teacher clarity has the potential to dramatically increase student achievement.

Fendick (1990) described teacher clarity as "a measure of the clarity of communication between teachers and students in both directions" (p. 10). He identified four dimensions of clarity:

1. **Clarity of organization** occurs when instructional topics, assignments, and objectives are aligned to learning.

2. **Clarity of explanation** occurs when the content and directions are clear.

3. **Clarity of examples and guided practice** happens when there is time for practice, clear explanation and feedback, and gradual release of instructional support.

4. **Clarity of assessment of student learning** occurs when teachers are regularly seeking and receiving feedback from students through verbal and written work.

Achievement Teams plan for clarity by developing learning progressions and short-cycle formative assessments before the first meeting cycle even takes place. Here are some of the benefits of such planning:

- Developing **learning progressions** sets a focused direction for teaching and learning. Clear progressions provide a pathway of incremental progress toward learning goals.
- Gaining **clarity of assessment** better equips teachers to understand how to use evidence to measure student learning. Students who develop the skill of self-evaluation become assessment capable—that is, learners who can diagnose their own strengths and needed next steps.
- In a learner-centered classroom that combines **clarity and feedback**, teachers and students understand the reciprocal nature of exchanging evidence-based information. Teachers use feedback to close the learning gap and answer the question, Where to next? (Hattie, 2012).

Planning for clarity is crucial (see Figure 2.1). It's a prerequisite that prepares teams for the collaborative process of the cycle.

## Selecting Essential Learning Targets

One of the biggest challenges for today's educators is how to navigate through an almost impossible number of learning targets to teach in one instructional year. Add to this an abundance of scripted lesson plans coupled with hyper-pacing guides, and you have an atmosphere of superficial coverage devoid of any depth of learning. Essential learning targets are not a new concept, and the idea of prioritizing them can certainly help eliminate frantic coverage of everything. Although some people use such terms as *standards, priority standards, power standards,* or *learning intentions,* we will refer to these items as *learning targets* for the purposes of this book.

**FIGURE 2.1**   Teacher Clarity and Achievement Teams

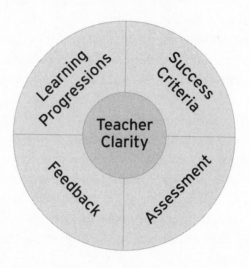

 **REFLECTION ACTIVITY**

Teacher Clarity

Is your team using learning progressions and short-cycle formative assessments? How are you using the results, or how might you use them to guide the direction of learning?

Essential learning targets, as the name implies, are a subset of skills and concepts identified as the most crucial learning for *all* students. They guide the development of common assessments, the focus for collaboration, and school-wide priorities. Formative assessments are the foundation for Achievement Teams, and we consistently remind practitioners that these short-cycle assessments are not intended to assess everything you teach. Rather, they focus on a few learning targets.

In terms of developing those targets, what's most important is the conversation that occurs among teachers. Teacher professional judgment and the selection of essential learning targets go a long way when it comes to making curricular decisions. School and district-level leaders need to keep the door open a little wider to listen to teacher voices and their ideas about prioritizing those targets.

The pacing of essential learning targets also helps determine the amount of instructional time that schools spend on high-impact targets. Many schools develop pacing calendars to ensure an equitable time for both teaching and learning. Rather than trying to compete with already established pacing guides, we recommend an assessment cycle that works within units of study.

Here are some common descriptions of the objective criteria used to select essential learning targets (Ainsworth, 2010):

- **Endurance** means that the learning students are exposed to lasts beyond a single year of instruction. Not all learning targets are created equal, and it's important to distinguish this difference, especially when we select learning targets that help prepare students for life, not just for a state test. For example, skills such as speaking and listening allow students to be successful communicators; summarizing, determining, and analyzing are all skills that enable students to be critical thinkers and transfer skills to real life.
- **Leverage** typically means that learning targets may support interdisciplinary connections among math, science, social studies, and language arts. For example, learning targets in writing can help bridge these gaps and encourage student written compositions as an integral part of all disciplines.
- **Readiness** is a prerequisite skill students need to succeed in another course of study or in the following grade level. Many learning targets are vertically aligned or scaffolded and represent learning progressions that happen over many years of school, not just a single lesson.

**REFLECTION ACTIVITY**

### Essential Learning Target Criteria

Various criteria can help identify essential learning targets. We've listed some of the guidelines that experts use in the areas of standards and assessment. As you reflect on the table below, consider what criteria determine the essential learning targets in your school or district.

| Ainsworth (2003) | Popham (2003) | Heflebower et al. (2014) | Criteria Used by Your District/School |
|---|---|---|---|
| • Endurance<br>• Leverage<br>• Readiness<br>• External exams | • Essential<br>• Highly desirable | • Endurance<br>• Leverage<br>• Readiness<br>• Teacher judgment<br>• Assessment | |

## The Rationale for Learning Progressions

Let's compare prerequisite instruction, or progressions, to a task such as learning to ride a bike. Before children learn how to balance on two wheels, they typically start with a tricycle. From there, they might progress to a balance bike with no pedals, with their feet on the ground. The next progression might be a transition to a bike with training wheels, which provides the necessary support to keep them from falling. After these sequenced experiences, the last progression would be the ability to balance on two wheels with no assistance. These building blocks of instruction help a child acquire the skills necessary to ride a bike with proper balance and forward momentum. Most important, children learn differently and may respond to some methods better than others. This example illustrates the rationale for incorporating learning progressions as part of the Achievement Teams framework.

Creating learning progressions has been one of the most successful areas of our training. To be clear, learning progressions are not the same as success criteria. *Success criteria* "provide the way of knowing that the desired learning intention has been achieved" (Hattie, 2009, p. 170). Teachers use *learning progressions* as they create and then teach a sequence of instructional steps. As the process of simple to complex instruction becomes clear, teachers attending Achievement Teams professional development sessions experience that moment of clarity and that feeling of discovery, and we facilitators immediately see the lightbulbs turn on. It's rewarding to observe teachers work through the process of breaking their essential learning targets into teachable chunks of instruction.

As teachers begin to create their learning progressions, they will list the prerequisite skills the students will need to begin to tackle the target. We know that teachers have limited time to teach all of their grade-level learning targets, so there may be a tendency to rush through instruction. Learning progressions permit teachers to incrementally introduce those building blocks of instruction that provide clarity for both teachers and students.

We cannot assume that students all have the same level of understanding. The fact is, they will have differing instructional starting points. By reviewing the prerequisite skills necessary to achieve the standard, teachers can introduce a learning target and then step up to another progression based on the cognitive rigor of that target.

## Defining Learning Progressions

The following definitions of learning progressions create a collective understanding of this essential instructional strategy:

- "Learning progressions represent prerequisite knowledge and skills that students must acquire incrementally before they are able to understand and apply more complex or advanced concepts and skills." (Ainsworth, 2015, p. 178)
- "Learning progressions are sequenced 'building blocks' of instruction that lead students to understand the unit learning targets. Look at each unit learning intention to decide what increments of instruction students will need to fully understand that learning intention. Then sequence these instructional building blocks in the order they will occur during the unit." (Ainsworth, 2015, p. 178)

- Learning progressions are "a set of building blocks—subskills and bodies of enabling knowledge—to be achieved by students on their way to mastering a target curricular aim." (Popham, 2008, p. 25)

- Learning progressions are vertically sequenced steps to acquire expertise pertaining to skills, knowledge, or dispositions within a specific domain. This sequence uses the concepts of continuity and coherence. "Learning is not viewed as a series of discrete events, but rather as a trajectory of development over time in a vertical fashion connecting knowledge, concepts, and skills within a domain over multiple grade levels." (Heritage, 2008)

- "Learning progressions describe in words and examples what it means to move over time toward more expert understanding. Learning progressions depict successively more sophisticated ways of thinking about an idea that might reasonably follow one another as students learn." (Nichols, 2010)

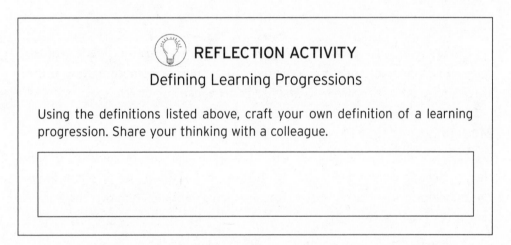

**REFLECTION ACTIVITY**

Defining Learning Progressions

Using the definitions listed above, craft your own definition of a learning progression. Share your thinking with a colleague.

## How to Create a Learning Progression

Achievement Teams use learning targets within a grade level to begin the process of creating sequenced instruction. Think of each step as a micro-progression leading to the overall learning target. The following steps will jump-start the learning progression stages by helping you create a list of specific criteria to consider as you begin this activity.

1. Select a single learning target of focus. Rigorous learning targets may offer more opportunities for sequencing. Before beginning this work, look at an entire

K–12 learning progression map because they're commonly developed based on the learning targets.

2. List what students need to do (as skills, so use verbs) and what they need to know (as concepts, so use nouns) to achieve the learning target.

3. Using Webb's Depth of Knowledge (DOK) tool (see Figure 2.2), design simple to complex instruction of a grade-level learning target.

4. Look for words or phrases you may need to define or identify (these are the prerequisite skills).

5. Before instruction, consider how struggling students typically think about this topic. This consideration will help you complete prerequisite planning.

6. Look for multiple concepts that you can break down into single concepts or steps.

7. Beginning with those lower-level skills, order each progression in a sequence that leads the student to the more complex skills contained within the learning target.

8. Remember, each progression builds on previous learning.

There's no single correct method for creating a progression. If the sequence selected is consistent with the next level of learning, then the progression itself will represent the steps necessary that lead to the learning target.

## Modeling Learning Progressions

Over the next few pages, we will model the learning progression process, then present an activity for you to try on your own. Learning progressions are the building blocks that teachers use to teach students the skills to master the learning target. Learning progressions

1. Represent a sequence of instruction, from simple to complex.
2. Identify prerequisite skills necessary to acquire the learning target.
3. Detail specific chunks of instruction.
4. Provide the foundation for short-cycle formative assessment.
5. Permit teachers to accelerate instruction.

We have selected an English language arts learning target to model this process (see Figure 2.3, p. 38). The importance of this learning target is a determining factor for selection. Students who can determine ideas, analyze, and summarize will increase their understanding, improve their comprehension, promote their

**FIGURE 2.2**  Webb's Depth of Knowledge (DOK) Tool

| Recall/ Reproduction DOK 1 | Skill/Concept DOK 2 | Strategic Thinking DOK 3 | Extended Thinking DOK 4 |
|---|---|---|---|
| Recall a fact, information, or procedure | Use information or conceptual knowledge; requires two or more steps | Requires reasoning, developing a plan or a sequence of steps; involves some complexity | Requires an investigation, time to think and process multiple conditions of the problem |
| • Arrange<br>• Define<br>• Describe who, what, where, when, or how<br>• Explain<br>• Identify<br>• Illustrate<br>• Label<br>• Locate<br>• Match<br>• Measure<br>• Name<br>• Perform<br>• Recall<br>• Recite<br>• Recognize<br>• Restate<br>• Solve one-step task<br>• Tell<br>• Use rules | • Apply<br>• Calculate<br>• Classify<br>• Construct simple model<br>• Describe/explain using context<br>• Determine<br>• Estimate<br>• Find<br>• Formulate<br>• Give examples and nonexamples<br>• Graph<br>• Identify patterns<br>• List several elements<br>• Perform a procedure<br>• Predict<br>• Solve multiple-step problems<br>• Summarize<br>• Use models to perform a procedure | • Analyze<br>• Argue<br>• Assess<br>• Cite evidence<br>• Compare<br>• Contrast<br>• Critique<br>• Decide<br>• Defend<br>• Distinguish<br>• Draw conclusions<br>• Explain how<br>• Extend patterns<br>• Formulate<br>• Infer<br>• Interpret<br>• Organize<br>• Outline<br>• Revise for meaning<br>• Show cause and effect<br>• Solve nonroutine problems<br>• Verify | • Apply concepts<br>• Create<br>• Collaborate<br>• Design and conduct<br>• Evaluate<br>• Formulate<br>• Generalize<br>• Hypothesize<br>• Initiate<br>• Produce/present<br>• Prove<br>• Reflect<br>• Reorganize into new structure<br>• Report<br>• Research |

*Note:* The DOK levels and descriptors are based on Norman Webb's Depth of Knowledge levels (1997).

critical thinking skills, and increase their use of writing strategies. This learning target contains three major skills:

- **Determine (DOK 2)**
- **Analyze (DOK 3)**
- **Summarize (DOK 2)**

**FIGURE 2.3**   English Language Arts Learning Target Example

As you see, each skill is assigned a DOK level based on Webb's Depth of Knowledge. This progression begins with lower-level prerequisite skills that lead to more rigorous skills, just like our analogy about learning to ride a bike. Lower-anchor instruction takes into consideration how struggling students may approach a specific learning target or skill. If we assume that students already know this material or that "they were taught this last year"—and they really haven't mastered it at all—then we deny them an opportunity to activate prior knowledge. On the other hand, if teachers discover that students possess more prior knowledge than anticipated, then they can accelerate instruction to an appropriate starting point. DOK levels are not developmental. All students can reach strategic thinking, no matter their age or grade.

Figure 2.4 shows how to develop the learning progressions using this same sample learning target. The first five progressions teach students prerequisite skills before they move on to the more complex skills (progressions 6–11). In other words, before we ask students to "determine two or more central ideas in a text," they may need instruction in what *determine* and *central idea* mean.

The thinking behind these micro-progressions is to capture an entire staircase to complexity by considering a few key points:

1. Look for words or phrases that you may need to define or identify (progressions 1–5).

2. Look for multiple concepts that you can break down into single concepts or steps (progressions 6 and 7).

**FIGURE 2.4**   Learning Progressions Planner

**Directions:** In the planner below, list what students should be able to do (skills/verbs) and know (concepts/nouns) to achieve the learning target. Use Figure 2.2, Webb's DOK Tool, to help you identify a progression of rigor from simple to complex.

**Learning Target:** Determine two or more central ideas in a text and analyze their development over the course of the text; provide an objective summary of the text.

| Steps | Skills (verbs) | Concepts (nouns and noun phrases) |
|:-----:|----------------|-----------------------------------|
| 1 | Define (DOK 1)... | *determine.* |
| 2 | Define (DOK 1)... | *analyze.* |
| 3 | Define (DOK 1)... | *summarize.* |
| 4 | Define (DOK 1)... | *central idea.* |
| 5 | Identify (DOK 1)... | *objective summary.* |
| 6 | Use text details to **determine (DOK 1)**... | a <u>single central idea</u> in a text. |
| 7 | Use text details to **analyze (DOK 3)**... | the development of a <u>single central idea</u> in a text. |
| 8 | Use text details to **determine (DOK 2)**... | <u>two or more central ideas</u> in a text. |
| 9 | Use text details to **analyze (DOK 3)**... | the development of <u>two or more central ideas</u> in a text. |
| 10 | Use text details to **provide an objective summary (DOK 2)**... | of a <u>single central idea</u> in a text. |
| 11 | Use text details to **provide an objective summary (DOK 2)**... | of <u>two or more central ideas</u> in a text. |
| 12 | Use text details to **provide an objective summary (DOK 2)**... | of the text. |

3. Confirm that all of the learning progressions contain the necessary building blocks of instruction to meet the entire learning target.

The value of learning progressions is immense:

1. They provide clarity for short-cycle pre- and post-assessments.
2. They give every student an opportunity to move from lower-level skills to upper-level and cognitively demanding skills.
3. They permit teachers to gain valuable information on appropriate starting points of instruction.
4. They represent an optimum sequence of instruction so students can demonstrate proficiency.

 **REFLECTION ACTIVITY**

## Learning Progressions

Now it's time for some independent practice. We have selected another English language arts learning target for you to consider:

**Learning target:** Cite several pieces of textual evidence to support your analysis of what the text says explicitly, as well as the inferences you have drawn from the text.

As you work through it, refer to the learning progression steps on pages 35–36. Should you prefer another learning target, choose your own or choose among our samples at www.steveventura.com/achievement-teams/resources-from-the-book.php. Figure 2.5 offers a blank learning progressions planner for you to use in this activity.

**Don't forget to refer to the look-fors:**
• Words or phrases that you may need to define or identify (these are considered the prerequisite skills)
• Multiple concepts that you can break down into single concepts or steps
• Subskills that precede more complex learning

**FIGURE 2.5**  Blank Learning Progressions Planner

**Directions:** In the planner below, list what students should be able to do (skills/verbs) and know (concepts/nouns) to achieve the learning target. Use Figure 2.2, Webb's DOK Tool, to help you identify a progression of rigor from simple to complex.

**Learning Target: Cite** several pieces of textual evidence to support your **analysis** of what the text says explicitly as well as the **inferences** you have drawn from the text.

| Steps | Skills (verbs) | Concepts (nouns and noun phrases) |
|:---:|---|---|
| 1 | | |
| 2 | | |
| 3 | | |
| 4 | | |
| 5 | | |
| 6 | | |
| 7 | | |
| 8 | | |
| 9 | | |
| 10 | | |
| 11 | | |
| 12 | | |

Learning Progressions and Leadership Teams

Because learning progressions can alter the rigor of classroom instruction and have a dramatic effect on student learning, school leaders must be clear on how to implement and monitor their use through the Achievement Teams process. They need to empower lead teachers to guide the process of developing clarity (through learning progressions, success criteria, and learning targets) in the school and classroom. For teachers to do this, they need continuous opportunities to collaborate. Moreover, teams need content experts to facilitate and guide conversations during the work sessions.

Learning progressions help create a more intentional pathway to the desired learning target. In addition, sequencing instruction helps develop teachers who can see potential in creating a set of prerequisite instructional strategies that lead to more rigorous skills and concepts. These chunks of instruction build grade-level capacity, assist students in self-regulating their own learning, and create opportunities for focused collaboration around student progress and around how to accelerate instruction. Finally, teachers gain information about their students' progress that can help create opportunities for differentiated instructional strategies.

The best way to include learning progressions in common school practice is to incorporate a learning progressions framework. In Achievement Teams, we stress the value of creating micro-progressions for a single learning target, encouraging teachers to unwrap standards using a simple-to-complex format of instruction. We begin with "granular progressions" that teachers can teach at the beginning of a learning target that ultimately level up to the learning target or goal.

To best support your Achievement Teams as they delve into this work, consider the following questions:

1. Does each team have a content expert? Which teachers have expertise in which subject areas?
2. How well do teams know and understand Webb's Depth of Knowledge? Hess's Cognitive Rigor Matrix? What type of support do they need to become familiar with these constructs?
3. How much time can teams devote to the first phase of developing learning progressions? To future phases?
4. What professional development do teachers need to further their knowledge?

As schools and districts encourage the use of learning progressions, leaders should recognize that the people most capable of creating effective progressions are the teachers themselves.

# What Are Success Criteria?

Developing learning targets and success criteria helps narrow the focus of instruction by identifying what matters most to student learning. It also enables teachers to align instruction with assessments. By using learning targets and success criteria in the classroom, students become self-regulated learners who perform up to two times more proficiently than students who rely on teacher support (Hattie, 2009).

Students who receive this kind of clarity in the classroom become better consumers of the content. They begin to think metacognitively about their work rather than always looking to the teacher for answers to challenging questions. Success criteria provide students with a model against which they can compare their own work and reflect on their learning. As Fisher, Frey, and Hattie (2016) note, "Showing students, near the beginning of a series of lessons, what success at the end should look like is among the more powerful things we can do to enhance learning" (p. 22).

Clearly articulated success criteria can lead to better feedback between teachers and students. They help create focus for students and provide them with opportunities to identify areas of strength and need. Once teachers create learning progressions and teach them to students, the criteria for success are a result of those progressions. Above all, teachers must purposely link success criteria to a specific learning target so students can demonstrate that they can monitor their own progress.

## Tips for Creating Success Criteria

After conducting dozens of sessions around the creation of success criteria, we have become acutely aware of some notable misconceptions. To clarify, we're going to work through success criteria using the following learning target:

> **Learning target: Determine** two or more central ideas in a text and **analyze** their development over the course of the text; provide an objective **summary** of the text.

One of the most common missteps when formulating success criteria is to simply repeat the learning target in the success criteria:

1. **Determine** two or more central ideas in a text.
2. **Analyze** their development over the course of the text.
3. Provide an objective **summary** of the text.

At first glance, you may think that these three criteria represent an accurate description of what students must do to demonstrate proficiency, and in a way, you'd be correct. After all, they contain the skills and concepts exactly as they appear in the target. However, crafting success criteria actually involves additional planning. As Hattie (2017) explains, "Effective teachers start with a standard, break the learning that standard requires into lesson-sized chunks, and then phrase these chunks so that students will be able to understand them" (p. 41).

Following this recommendation from Hattie, we see opportunities to create success criteria that provide additional clarity for students. Rather than repeating the learning target, the success criteria must be explicit and be written as "I can" statements from the students' point of view, such as in the following example:

**Success Criteria**
1. I can state (determine) two central ideas of the text.
2. I can identify at least two key details for each central idea.
3. I can analyze the details to explain how they support the central ideas.
4. I can formulate an objective summary of the text, including the central ideas and their development.

Figure 2.6 compares a "good" and a "better" version of success criteria. The left-hand column contains a generic form of success criteria, whereas the right-hand column breaks the success criteria down into more granular chunks. Also, note that the success criteria (*determine, analyze,* and *summarize*) reflect the skills highlighted in the learning target, what students need to do to reach proficiency. This is especially important because you should not write success criteria in a way that lowers their rigor or complexity. We cannot ask students to *analyze* and *summarize* if we only teach them to *identify* and *describe*.

Here's an example from social studies, which includes the learning target and success criteria:

> **Learning target:** Describe the contribution of Roman civilization to law, literature, poetry, architecture, engineering, and technology (for example, roads, bridges, arenas, baths, aqueducts, central heating, plumbing, and sanitation).

This particular learning target asks students to describe many different contributions of Roman civilization, but we chose to narrow it down to one—technology.

**Success Criteria**

- I can state accurately a technological contribution.
- I can describe (explain) how the contribution improved a Roman's daily life.
- I can include 2–3 sentences in my explanation.
- I can make a connection to my own personal experience: How has this contribution improved my life?

Once you've crafted the success criteria for a technological contribution, you can substitute any of the other contributions without drastically altering the overall criteria for success. For example, in place of "I can state accurately a technological contribution," you might choose any of the following:

- I can state accurately how Roman civilization contributed to the legal system and law.
- I can state accurately how Roman civilization contributed to literature.
- I can state accurately how Roman civilization contributed to architecture.

You might also think about adding other criteria that were not necessarily listed in the original learning intention but that add value to the student learning experience. In our example about Rome, the fourth success criterion asks students to make a personal connection to their own life ("How has this contribution improved my life?"). Because the engineering and technological innovations developed in ancient Rome are still very much a part of the technological issues we face today, it seems logical to ask students to make this connection.

**FIGURE 2.6**  Learning Target and Success Criteria: Good and Better

| Learning Target: **Determine** two or more central ideas in a text and **analyze** their development over the course of the text; provide an objective **summary** of the text. | |
|---|---|
| **Good** | **Better** |
| ☐ **Determine** two or more central ideas in a text.<br>☐ **Analyze** their development over the course of the text.<br>☐ **Provide** an objective summary of the text. | ☐ State (**determine**) two central ideas of the text.<br>☐ Identify at least two key details for each central idea.<br>☐ **Analyze** the details to explain how they support the central ideas.<br>☐ Formulate an objective **summary** of the text, including the central ideas and their development. |

### Rubrics and Scoring Guides

Teachers can easily add success criteria into rubrics and proficiency scales to assist in determining student progress. A holistic scoring guide is one commonly used rubric. Craig A. Mertler (2001) of Bowling Green State University defines holistic scoring guides as "a process that permits teachers to score the overall process or product as a whole" (p. 1). Using holistic rubrics, which give students a single overall score, can result in a somewhat quicker scoring process than using analytic rubrics (Nitko, 2001), which require teachers to try to fit students into appropriate levels. Holistic rubrics provide more clarity and better feedback than analytic rubrics.

Figure 2.7 shows a holistic scoring guide for the social studies learning target about Rome. Holistic scoring guides are relatively easy to create and use. We usually create the Achieving criteria first, followed by the Excelling criteria, which indicate that the student must satisfy all the Achieving criteria—*plus.* Our Progressing and Beginning criteria are based on the number of tasks that the student still needs to achieve.

**FIGURE 2.7**  Holistic Scoring Guide for a Social Studies Learning Target

| **Excelling:** Demonstrates all three Achieving success criteria, plus… | • Makes a connection to a personal experience |
|---|---|
| **Achieving:** Demonstrates all three success criteria | • States accurately a technological contribution<br>• Explains how the contribution improved a Roman's daily life<br>• Includes 2–3 sentences in the explanation |
| **Progressing:** | • Demonstrates two of the Achieving success criteria |
| **Beginning:** | • Demonstrates fewer than two of the Achieving success criteria |

Another way to think of success criteria is to split up the target into categories and address each one individually, as in the following example:

Learning target: Explain the function of conjunctions, prepositions, and interjections in general and their function in a particular sentence.

### Success Criteria for Conjunctions
- I can identify a correlative conjunction in a sentence.
- I can explain the conjunction set's purpose or meaning.
- I can use the conjunction set in my writing and speaking.

### Success Criteria for Prepositions
- I can identify a preposition in a sentence when speaking.
- I can explain the preposition's meaning.
- I can use the preposition in my writing and speaking.

### Success Criteria for Interjections
- I can identify an interjection in a sentence.
- I can explain why an interjection is being used.
- I can use an interjection in my writing and speaking.

Success criteria should prompt students to *find, write, solve, create*—to do some action that reflects the content of the learning target. This helps students understand what they are to learn. Figure 2.8 shows some verbs you can use with criteria for success.

**FIGURE 2.8**  Success Criteria Verbs

**Success criteria typically use verbs like...**

| | | |
|---|---|---|
| Explain | Solve | Compare |
| Describe | Graph | Contrast |
| Model | Find | Calculate |
| Show | Measure | Locate |
| Write | Label | Name |
| Create | Restate | Construct |

## Content Chunking Using Success Criteria

Content chunking is an excellent strategy because it combines smaller chunks of learning with success criteria and provides multiple opportunities for learners to recall information that is delivered in more manageable, bite-size pieces. Content chunking has its roots in a paper written in 1956 by cognitive psychologist George

A. Miller of Harvard University. Miller suggested that chunking makes more effective use of our short-term memory because the information taught is organized by grouping various pieces of information together.

Figure 2.9 illustrates how learning progressions and success criteria can fit neatly into a content chunking map. Instruction is broken down into four subtopics, with topics 1A and 2A featuring prerequisite knowledge and skills and topics 1B and 2B featuring advanced skills and concepts. From here, it's possible to create success criteria based on smaller pieces of instruction.

**FIGURE 2.9**  Content Chunking

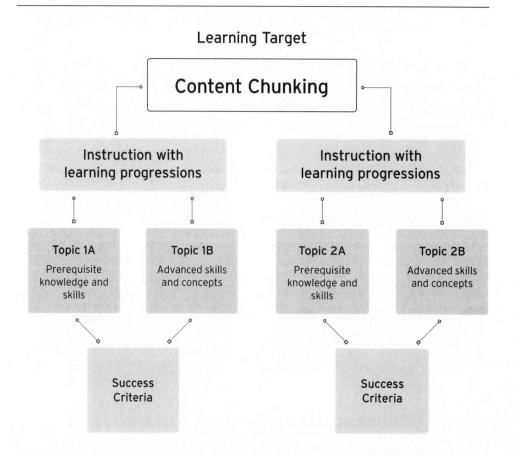

Success criteria are most effective when they

- Are co-constructed and shared with students.
- Are used by students to evaluate their own work.
- Use kid-friendly language.
- Are clearly articulated.
- Are referred to often throughout the lesson.
- Are visible throughout the lesson.
- Purposely link to a specific learning intention.

Success criteria clarify what students must learn by giving them clear explanations and demonstrations. In addition, they help sequence lessons and activities in a logical and clearly delineated format. By developing success criteria between the pre- and post-assessments, teachers enable students to acquire mastery and to clearly understand the learning target.

Figure 2.10 clarifies the difference between learning progressions (top) and success criteria (bottom). Learning progressions are the instructional steps teachers create to teach the learning target, and success criteria are the results of the progression and instruction.

## Key Takeaways

- Teacher clarity is a framework built on collaborative philosophies and explicit instruction and is a prerequisite to forming Achievement Teams.
- Essential learning targets, also called standards or learning intentions, are the skills and concepts identified as the most crucial learning for *all* students.
- Using learning progressions can alter the rigor of classroom instruction and dramatically affect student learning.
- Developing learning targets and success criteria enables teachers to align instruction with assessments.

**FIGURE 2.10** Learning Progressions Versus Success Criteria

**Learning Progressions, Steps 1–12**

| Steps | Skills (verbs) | Concepts (nouns and noun phrases) |
|---|---|---|
| 1 | Define (DOK 1)… | *determine.* |
| 2 | Define (DOK 1)… | *analyze.* |
| 3 | Define (DOK 1)… | *summarize.* |
| 4 | Define (DOK 1)… | *central idea.* |
| 5 | Identify (DOK 1)… | *objective summary.* |
| 6 | Use text details to **determine (DOK 1)**… | a <u>single central idea</u> in a text. |
| 7 | Use text details to **analyze (DOK 3)**… | the development of a <u>single central idea</u> in a text. |
| 8 | Use text details to **determine (DOK 2)**… | <u>two or more central ideas</u> in a text. |
| 9 | Use text details to **analyze (DOK 3)**… | the development of <u>two or more central ideas</u> in a text. |
| 10 | Use text details to **provide an objective summary (DOK 2)**… | of a <u>single central idea</u> in a text. |
| 11 | Use text details to **provide an objective summary (DOK 2)**… | of <u>two or more central ideas</u> in a text. |
| 12 | Use text details to **provide an objective summary (DOK 2)**… | of the text. |

**A Learning Target with Its Success Criteria**

**Learning Target:** Determine two or more central ideas in a text and analyze their development over the course of the text; provide an objective summary of the text.

I can

1. State (determine) two central ideas in a text.
2. Identify at least two key details for each central idea.
3. Analyze the details to explain how they support the central ideas.
4. Formulate an objective summary of the text, including the central ideas and their development.

# 3

# Clarity of Assessment

*Only when you know how a student's knowledge or beliefs have shifted can you begin to identify the effect of specific activities (teaching).*

—Graham Nuthall

When we speak of clarity, we're also referring to *clarity of assessment*. It's important to differentiate among the major forms of assessment that schools commonly use, all of which offer different levels of interpretation.

## Three Kinds of Assessments

Members of Achievement Teams need to know what constitutes high-quality assessment and how to differentiate among the following three kinds:

1. **Summative assessments** are typically associated with end-of-year state testing, and the results are designed to measure student proficiency as compared to specific criteria, such as learning targets. These standardized tests are associated with a state accountability system and are not designed to provide teachers with timely information about student learning.

2. **Interim assessments** may be administered between formative and summative assessments, and they are more commonly referred to as *benchmark assessments*. Although these assessments occur more frequently than summative assessments do, the frequency of administration is limited. They do assist teachers with identifying skills and concepts that students are struggling to learn, but time may be lacking to correct those errors.

3. **Formative assessments** are ongoing, short-cycle assessments that provide teachers and students with timely information about student performance strengths and gaps. They can also provide teachers with information about who they taught effectively and who needs more help. Formative assessments also improve professional practice by providing teachers with a continuous process of

gathering evidence and making inferences, all designed to promote higher levels of student achievement.

Hattie and Timperley (2007) stress that formative assessment has proven beneficial when it comes to informing instruction, closing achievement gaps, and preparing students for additional assessment. In the absence of formative assessment opportunities for all students, the probability of maintaining status-quo achievement and of regressing student growth may increase.

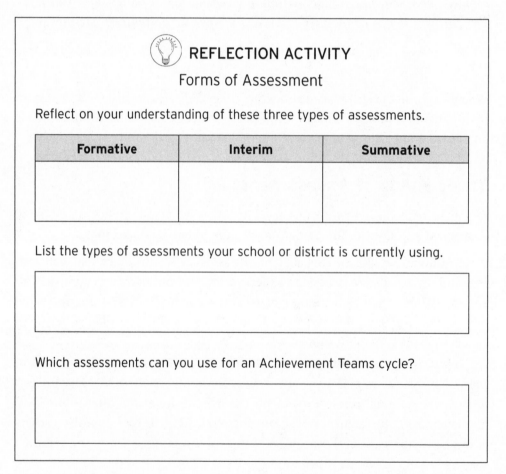

**REFLECTION ACTIVITY**
Forms of Assessment

Reflect on your understanding of these three types of assessments.

| Formative | Interim | Summative |
|-----------|---------|-----------|
|           |         |           |

List the types of assessments your school or district is currently using.

Which assessments can you use for an Achievement Teams cycle?

## Formative Assessment and Achievement Teams

Formative assessment can accelerate the speed of learning (Hattie, 2009). It's also one of the critical components of Achievement Teams, along with goals, feedback, and response to intervention (RTI). (Note that although RTI is included as one of the six critical components, a full discussion of RTI is beyond the scope of this book.) These other components would lose their impact without formative assessment.

Frequent assessment is powerful because it guides the teaching and learning process and helps create what Hattie calls *adaptive learning experts* (2009, 2012). According to Hattie, adaptive experts can assess student needs throughout the learning process and make the necessary modifications to help them meet worthwhile learning goals. Formative assessment gives teachers the feedback they need to apply corrective instruction.

Achievement Teams incorporate the use of short-cycle assessments to guide teachers in focusing on the formative effects of their teaching. Teachers create valid and reliable assessments to help them reflect on their instructional efforts, rather than just focus on grading student results.

**Formative assessment should**
- Inform teacher practice.
- Promote equity for all students.
- Build the capacity of all team members.
- Provide an effective strategy to determine if students have achieved the learning targets.
- Offer a powerful tool to appropriate new knowledge about teaching and learning.
- Encourage students to become better consumers of their own learning.

In Achievement Teams, teachers review assessment results to determine not only how much students have learned, but also how to evaluate the effect of instruction. Assessing prior knowledge (diagnostic) is a good thing, *provided students have prior knowledge.* Traditional pre-assessment certainly plays an important role in the teaching-learning cycle, but it must also provide a way for teachers to gather key information about what students know and are able to do and about who was taught effectively and who still needs help. Many pre-assessments only affirm what teachers have already inferred—that students don't have enough prior knowledge to take a cold pre-assessment on new material. This is a waste of instructional time because the data collected don't challenge teachers. If there's no change in instruction, then the pre-assessment served no purpose. Pre-assessment results should enable teachers to provide timely feedback to students while evaluating the effects of teacher instruction. As you will see, Achievement Teams encourage the use of a "pre-teach/reteach" model of assessment to truly reflect on teacher impact.

In *10 Mindframes for Visible Learning* (2018), Hattie and Zierer present three mindframes that speak directly to the effective use of formative assessment on student learning:

- "I am an evaluator of my impact on student learning" (p. 1). It's the teacher's role to know their impact.
- "I see assessment as informing my impact and the next steps" (p. 12). Assessments are a reflection of the teacher's effort more than the students' effort.
- "I collaborate with my peers and my students about my conceptions of progress and my impact" (p. 24). Although teamwork is essential, adults aren't nearly as good at it as students.

It's our *thinking* about impact that's so crucial. As Hattie and Zierer point out, "How we think about the impact of what we do is more important than what we do" (p. ix). Also, as you can see, these three mindframes are all about evaluating impact, not just assessing and grading students.

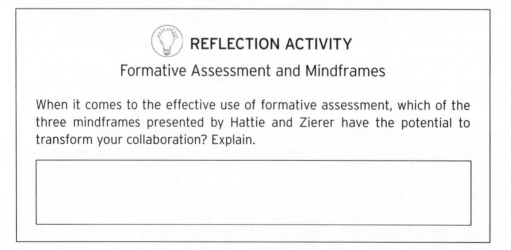

**REFLECTION ACTIVITY**

Formative Assessment and Mindframes

When it comes to the effective use of formative assessment, which of the three mindframes presented by Hattie and Zierer have the potential to transform your collaboration? Explain.

## Assessment and the Learner-Centered Classroom

Students in a learner-centered classroom view assessment as a process that provides information regarding progress toward goals. Teachers see assessment as a means to measure their effect and guide instructional decisions. For example, formative assessment helps teachers address four focus questions:

1. What strengths and gaps do the assessment results show?
2. What skills (verbs) and concepts (nouns and noun phrases) were achieved from the learning target, and what still needs to be learned?
3. Who did we teach effectively, and who still needs help?
4. Which instructional strategies were effective? Which ones were less effective?

In a student-centered classroom, students know the success criteria required to achieve the learning target. They will begin to think metacognitively and will be able to answer the following questions:

- Where am I now? What did I learn?
- What are my next steps?
- How am I going to reach my goal?

## Short-Cycle Assessments

Short-cycle assessments can take on many different meanings, so we want to be clear about how to use them in conjunction with Achievement Teams. Short-cycle assessments are pre- and post-assessments that teachers can administer anywhere from two to four weeks apart. Teachers often administer these before the end of a unit of instruction; they typically don't grade them because of their formative purpose. The assessments provide initial baseline information that teachers can use to create instructional planning for individual students as well as for an entire class. Further, they provide feedback about instructional success and enable teachers to answer the four focus questions noted above.

## Achievement Teams Assessment Options

Achievement Teams are most effective when we take advantage of a "pre-teach/reteach" model, rather than a cold, diagnostic "pre-/post-assessment" model, because the point is to enable teachers to apply corrective instruction before it's too late and to assess their instructional impact.

To clarify this concept, let's look at the difference between diagnostic assessment and a pre-teach/reteach assessment model.

### Diagnostic Assessment

Diagnostic pre-assessment helps reveal student prior knowledge. In many cases, teachers administer these assessments at the beginning of a unit of instruction or in preparation to teach new skills and concepts. Once they collect and analyze the results, they can use the information to adjust instruction to improve student achievement.

The diagram shown in Figure 3.1 describes this model. Discussion questions like "Who did we teach effectively?" and "What strategies were effective?" will likely have to wait until after the administration of the second assessment. And that's fine, as long as there's still time to apply corrective instruction.

**FIGURE 3.1**   The Diagnostic Assessment Model

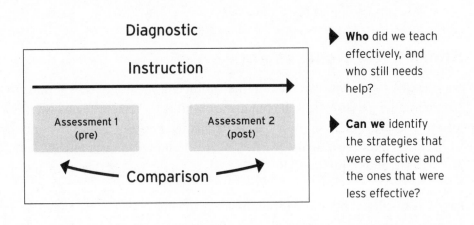

## Pre-Teach/Reteach Assessment

The pre-teach/reteach model (see Figure 3.2) permits teachers to introduce the skills and concepts to assess *before* administering the actual assessment. How much time you spend reviewing the material with students can vary based on the rigor of the learning target; however, providing students with that quick review may help produce accurate assessment results. Remember, if we truly want to measure whether our teaching is having the effect we want, then we must consider using an assessment model that is more reflective of the *instructional practices we're implementing* than of student effort. In a pre-teach/reteach model, teachers are more likely to address the questions "Who did we teach effectively?" and "What strategies were effective?" before the second assessment.

**FIGURE 3.2**   The Pre-Teach/Reteach Model

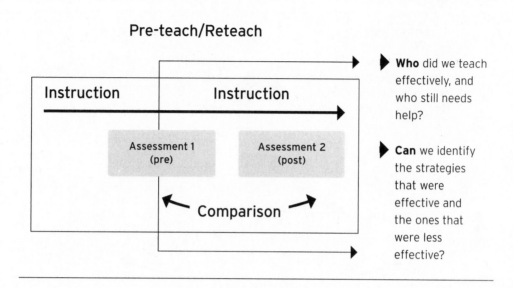

**Assessment Options: Mirrored or Aligned?**

In Achievement Teams, it's imperative that teachers develop pre- and post-assessments to complete a cycle. To determine student growth and teacher impact, these assessments are most effective when they're *mirrored* or *aligned*.

### Mirrored Assessment

Mirrored assessment permits teachers to make a direct comparison between two assessments because the assessments are essentially the same (see Figure 3.3). Mirrored assessments

1. Are administered under the same conditions (same level of complexity, content, use of technology or paper/pencil).

2. Contain the same number of problems.

3. Give students the same amount of time to complete both pre- and post-assessments.

This comparison is designed to measure change between two or more short-cycle assessments administered at different times. Teachers can use mirrored assessments to make accurate inferences by integrating reliable data and developing conclusions about student progress and instructional impact.

**FIGURE 3.3**  The Mirrored Assessment Model

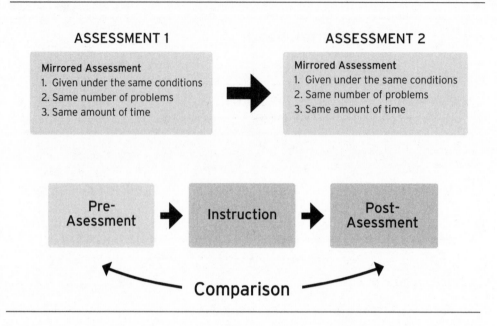

## Aligned Assessment

Aligned assessment offers a unique option between pre- and post-assessments in that teachers can take advantage of additional flexibility (see Figures 3.4 and 3.5). Aligned assessments

1. Are given under the same conditions (same level of complexity, content, use of technology or paper/pencil).

2. Contain fewer items on the pre-assessment and additional items on the post-assessment.

3. Include the original items from the pre-assessment on the post-assessment for comparison.

4. Provide students with more time to take the post-assessment because it contains additional items.

The additional items on the post-assessment might include new content that was taught between the pre- and the post-assessment. The comparison would only include the aligned items from both assessments. Sometimes teachers use the additional items on the post-assessment as a new pre-assessment.

**FIGURE 3.4**  The Aligned Assessment Model

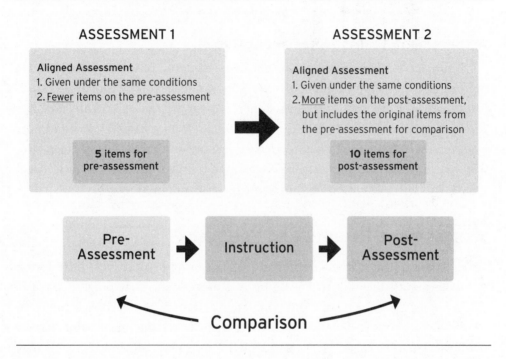

**FIGURE 3.5**  Mirrored Versus Aligned Assessments

| Mirrored Assessments | Aligned Assessments |
|---|---|
| • Are comparable in order to measure student growth between a pre- and post-assessment cycle | • Accurately match each other |
| • Are mostly identical | • Permit teachers to assess additional items included on the post-assessment |
| • Permit teachers to make accurate inferences based on a set of clearly identified assessment items | • Enable teachers to use additional items on the post-assessment as a possible pre-assessment for a new pre- and post-assessment cycle |

Either assessment cycle, mirrored or aligned, will enhance your Achievement Teams meetings, but to truly reap the benefits of Achievement Teams assessment, we must incorporate a *pre- and post-assessment cycle* to determine the instructional impact and student progress. As assessment guru James Popham (2003) put it, "The improvement between the pretests and posttests constitutes credible evidence of the teachers' instructional success" (para. 30). So let's now look at assessment cycles.

### Achievement Teams Assessment Cycles

Figure 3.6 depicts three options for an assessment cycle: two offer pre-teach options and reteaching buffers; the third is the more conventional approach, featuring just a pre- and post-assessment. The graphic can assist team members with initial assessment calendar ideas, including selecting dates for pre- and post-assessments. Although there's no perfect time frame for assessment, there is value in connecting the teaching/learning cycle to the timing of these short-cycle assessments. This will make meeting time more meaningful and focused.

## Assessment Results and Feedback

When students and teachers understand the meaning behind short-cycle formative assessments, they see that learning is a process and that progress has true value when you can measure and celebrate it. Here's where feedback comes in. Leadership expert Ken Blanchard (2015) calls feedback "the breakfast of champions"; Margaret Heritage (2011) refers to it as "instructional action." Teams need to study this critical component because, as Hattie (2009) explains, it can double the speed of learning.

Providing feedback and assessment results is an important function of Achievement Teams. For you to close the gaps you've discovered from pre-assessment results, your students are likely going to require feedback that explains to them where they are and where they need to be. In fact, feedback is much more effective when it helps students make connections to their own prior learning and effort.

According to Hattie and Timperley's (2007) model, feedback can occur at four levels:

1. **Task level.** This level includes feedback about how well the student is accomplishing or performing a given task.

2. **Process level.** This level includes feedback about the processes underlying the tasks or about relating and extending tasks.

3. **Self-regulation level.** This type of feedback helps students monitor, direct, and regulate their actions toward the learning goal.

4. **Self level.** This level usually consists of praise, so for our purposes here, we'll focus on levels 1–3.

**FIGURE 3.6**   Sample Three-Week Assessment Cycle

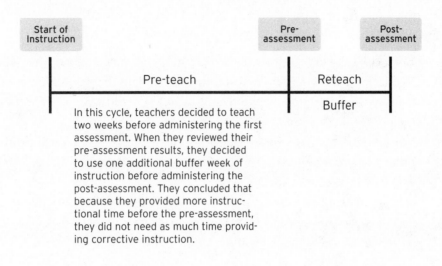

In this cycle, teachers decided to teach two weeks before administering the first assessment. When they reviewed their pre-assessment results, they decided to use one additional buffer week of instruction before administering the post-assessment. They concluded that because they provided more instructional time before the pre-assessment, they did not need as much time providing corrective instruction.

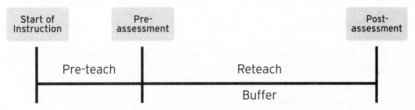

In this cycle, teachers decided to teach one week before administering the pre-assessment. When they reviewed their pre-assessment results, they decided to use two* additional weeks of corrective instruction before administering the post-assessment.

*This sample uses a three-week cycle to demonstrate the advantages of a pre-teach/ reteach assessment model. We don't wish to suggest that three weeks is the perfect time between pre- and post-assessments. That should be determined by the level of rigor of the learning target and other factors based on teacher professional judgment.

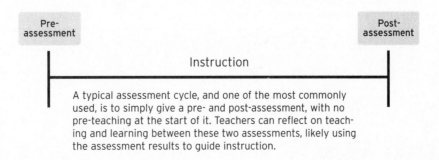

A typical assessment cycle, and one of the most commonly used, is to simply give a pre- and post-assessment, with no pre-teaching at the start of it. Teachers can reflect on teaching and learning between these two assessments, likely using the assessment results to guide instruction.

To determine which level of feedback is most appropriate for a given situation, think about the student's acquisition of new knowledge and skills. The type of feedback to provide depends on the level of instruction and learning. Here are some examples:

- **Task:** Use task-level feedback for new material. You can use this type of feedback for students who may have struggled with the pre-assessment (students at the Beginning or Progressing stage). A sample prompt for the task level of feedback would be, "What is the correct answer?"
- **Process:** Use process-level feedback when the student has *some* degree of proficiency. A sample prompt for this level of feedback would be, "Explain why that's the correct answer."
- **Self-Regulation:** Use self-regulation–level feedback when the student has a *high* degree of proficiency. A sample feedback prompt for this level of feedback would be, "What can you do differently next time?"

For additional sample feedback prompts, see Figure 3.7.

**FIGURE 3.7**   Sample Feedback-Level Prompts

**Task (for Beginning and Progressing students)**

**What is task-level feedback?**

The focus is on
- Distinguishing correct from incorrect answers.
- Acquiring more or different information.
- Building more surface knowledge.
- Reteaching and providing multiple opportunities to learn.

**What prompts can you use to offer task-level feedback?**
- Does your answer meet the success criteria?
- Is your answer correct/incorrect?
- How can you elaborate on the answer?
- What did you do well?
- Where did you go wrong?
- What is the correct answer?

**Process (for Achieving students)**

**What is process-level feedback?**

The focus is on
- Relationships among ideas.
- Students' strategies for error detection.
- Explicitly learning from errors.
- Cueing the learner to different strategies and errors.

**What prompts can you use to offer process-level feedback?**
- What is wrong and why?
- What strategies did you use?
- What is the explanation for the correct answer?
- What other questions can you ask about the task?
- What are the relationships with other parts of the task?

**Self-Regulation (for Achieving and Excelling students)**

**What is self-regulation feedback?**

The focus is on
- Being able to create internal feedback and self-assess.
- Being willing to invest effort in seeking and dealing with feedback information.
- Being able to review work to decide if an answer is correct.
- Knowing to seek help to find additional information or to confirm a response.

**What prompts can you use to offer self-regulation feedback?**
- How can you monitor your own work?
- How can you carry out self-checking?
- How can you evaluate the information provided?
- How can you reflect on your own learning?
- What did you do to _____?
- What might you do differently next time?
- How could you improve this work?

*Source:* From *Visible Learning for Teachers: Maximizing Impact on Learning* (p. 145) by J. Hattie, 2012, Routledge. © 2012 by John Hattie. Adapted with permission.

**REFLECTION ACTIVITY**

## Giving Feedback to Students

Using the prompts listed, reflect on your experiences giving and receiving feedback. Complete this on your own or with colleagues, and discuss your reflections.

| What types of effective feedback do you give students? | How do you know when your students need to move to the next level of feedback? | Does the feedback you give to students match the instructional level they are working at? | What *actions* do you take as a result of the feedback you give (task, process, self-regulation)? How do you modify your instruction? |
|---|---|---|---|
|  |  |  |  |

 Leading Assessment

Assessment drives the teaching and learning cycle, serves as an instructional guide, and informs teachers of the effect of their instruction. The results are most effective when teachers use assessments *during* instruction rather than at the end of a unit or course of study. We encourage Achievement Team members to interpret assessment results as an assessment of teacher effort by incorporating a pre-teach/reteach assessment cycle.

Summative assessment is so prevalent in today's schools that we often wonder if we're placing enough emphasis on formative assessment and evaluation. Because Achievement Teams use formative assessment throughout every cycle, leaders need to understand the continuous nature of the process.

James Popham (2008) refers to formative assessment as a "planned process" because teachers use the results to adjust both teaching and learning. When leaders work with teams and PLCs, it can be challenging for them to keep the "formative" in the assessment process because so many are accustomed to summative cycles. Formative assessment is a continuous process: you close learning gaps and expose new ones, and this happens over and over again (Heritage, 2010).

 **REFLECTION ACTIVITY**

## Planning for Short-Cycle Assessment Implementation

Talk with your leadership team, and determine what actions need to be taken to support your school with effective implementation of assessment literacy and Achievement Teams.

| Assessment Component | Action Needed to Implement |
|---|---|
| Common formative assessment | |
| Achievement Teams assessment options (diagnostic or pre-teach/reteach) | |
| Building capacity—assessment literacy | |
| Monitoring the quality of assessment items | |

Assessment Literacy for Leaders

Leading an assessment cycle means clarifying the value and purpose of formative assessment. First, leaders need to explain the differences between benchmark and formative assessments. Well-intentioned schools and districts make claims to formative assessment implementation, but they administer these assessments at the end of a quarter or unit. This is summative assessment.

Formative assessments take place during an instructional unit, and they're typically not graded. The results enable teachers to make instructional adjustments and mid-course corrections *before the end of the unit*.

We do want to be clear about benchmark or interim assessments. They're an integral part of an assessment system, but they prove most effective when they're designed to support short-cycle formative assessment.

To support formative assessment and Achievement Teams, leaders can consider some implementation options that will lead to quick wins. For example, if you're looking to create clarity and focus in an elementary school setting, consider implementing Achievement Teams focused on one content area—for example, language arts or mathematics.

This strategy can

• Familiarize teachers with developing short-cycle assessments and build support.

• Create a degree of consistency.

• Permit teachers to spend more time on instruction that is designed to increase student achievement as opposed to creating multiple content-area assessments in an academic year.

Secondary schools can take advantage of these strategies as well by starting with a single prep or class. Focus trumps superficial coverage every time.

## What Matters

Schools can enjoy greater success with Achievement Teams implementation when leaders and teachers work together to create regular and frequent opportunities to discuss and analyze short-cycle assessment results. This works best when teachers have time to collaborate in grade-level or department teams.

# Key Takeaways

- When teams have clarity about learning targets and assessment, they're better equipped to meet the needs of all students and provide learning experiences that are engaging, equitable, and meaningful.
- Feedback must be relevant and effective for students to progress and use the feedback to grow their learning.
- Developing a positive school culture and clear curricular structure provides the foundational components needed to begin the Achievement Teams process.

# 4

# Planning for Achievement Teams

*Having clarity about the big picture before diving into
the details supports a more efficient curriculum design process.*

—Heidi Hayes Jacobs

Now that we have determined core practices and have created a foundation for implementation, we can drill down to explicit and practical micro-practices that lead to a cascade of success. Fundamental to achieving breakthrough results in student achievement are a commitment to teamwork and an openness to new strategies, as well as the participation of all staff in the effort.

We think we know the reason we're so inspired by teacher teams that continually achieve their goals: They believe that powerful collaboration is worth the time and effort. They realize that each cycle is an opportunity for a fresh start, and they continually find effective ways to work through challenges. Achievement Teams are more than just teacher meetings; they're partnerships where professionals can celebrate milestones, create innovative ways to approach teaching and learning, and promote opportunities to combine collective knowledge.

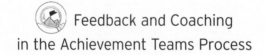 Feedback and Coaching
in the Achievement Teams Process

When talking about the importance of the role of the instructional leader during an event some years back, John Hattie (2009) asked, "How can I increase the amount of feedback I give teachers on their efforts toward increasing achievement?" He pointed out that providing feedback to teachers on the effect of their instructional efforts is second only to ensuring kids are safe and secure at school as the primary role of an instructional leader. Or as Grant Wiggins (2012) explains, "Feedback is also effective when it is connected to a goal because it makes the feedback more tangible" (p. 13). Without feedback, teachers may continue to use instructional strategies that don't work.

### Why the Urgency?

Hattie (2012) describes the vast variances in the effects that teachers have on students during their schooling. Students who receive instruction from a high-effect teacher, compared with a low-effect teacher, can expect almost a year's advantage in learning. He also discovered that the most significant variation in teaching lies within, not outside, the school—meaning that expertise varies among teachers within a single school setting. This is where Achievement Teams can be quite compelling, since they allow teachers to share expertise, strategies, and general knowledge around teaching and learning.

When educational leaders structure professional development so high-effect teachers can collaborate with their low-effect peers, teachers learn from one another and provide feedback and coaching. There *is* a need for urgency. For those of us administrators who used to observe a teacher's classroom and then leave a sticky note with positive comments on the teacher's desk, thinking all along that we were providing outstanding feedback, let us just point out that it's doubtful that sticky notes are going to close the instructional gap.

## Peer-to-Peer Feedback

The Achievement Teams protocol provides an opportunity for teachers to focus on increasing student achievement and analyzing student data. In Step 4 of our framework—select high-yield instructional strategies—the team uses a collaborative protocol to determine research-based strategies that will accelerate learning based on student needs. The teachers function as a learning team and consist of both expert and novice teachers.

Peer-to-peer feedback must be a two-way conversation. It can help teams look for best practices that can add value and contribute to the overall success of the meeting.

**REFLECTION ACTIVITY**

Peer Feedback for Growth

Think of a time you received difficult feedback from a peer. Did you receive the feedback positively, or did it frustrate you? Did the feedback help you grow? What norms need to be in place for us to give and receive feedback positively within a collaborative setting?

 Coaching and Feedback Models

Leaders have a twofold purpose in using Achievement Teams, PLCs, and data teams: (1) to increase student achievement and close learning gaps, and (2) to improve teachers' knowledge and skills. There's simply not enough time during a meeting to provide meaningful professional development or model a strategy well enough for deep implementation. However, *after* the meeting is an ideal time to extend professional learning in the form of coaching and feedback. As a leader, you can provide the necessary resources and support.

A variety of coaching models provide such support. For example, schools and districts use *instructional rounds* to better understand the quality of teaching and learning that occurs in classrooms (Elmore et al., 2009). Here, a group of educators makes a series of visits to multiple classrooms to observe what's taking place in the instructional core. This process enables educators to observe, gather data, collaborate, and reflect on instructional practice. Robert Marzano (2011) explains that the goal of instructional rounds isn't to provide feedback to the teacher, although this is an option if the observed teacher so desires. Rather, the primary purpose is for observing teachers to compare their own instructional practices with those of the teachers they observe. The chief benefit of this approach resides in the discussion that takes place among observing teachers at the end of the observation as well as in subsequent self-reflection.

Achievement Teams can use instructional rounds to further their understanding of instructional strategies and clarify how to use them in a deliberate and targeted manner. (This is tied to Step 3 in our protocol: Create baseline evidence statements.) Team members develop a shared understanding of the lesson through dialogue that occurs following the lesson. For this approach to work best, leaders and team members need to create an optimal adult learning environment that provides safety, empathy, feedback, and coaching.

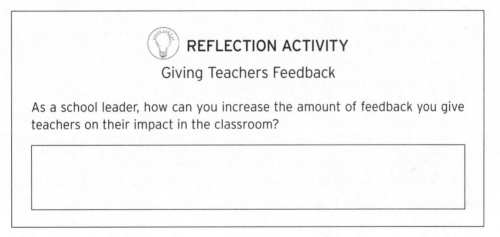

**REFLECTION ACTIVITY**

Giving Teachers Feedback

As a school leader, how can you increase the amount of feedback you give teachers on their impact in the classroom?

## Microteaching in the Feedback Process

Microteaching, a research-based strategy with roots in teacher training programs, was first used to improve knowledge and understanding of instructional practice. The term refers to practice teaching in which a student teacher's teaching of a small class is videotaped for subsequent evaluation. It's now a common strategy in schools because of its effect on student learning and its ease of use for teachers and teams. When used effectively and deliberately, microteaching can double the speed of learning (Hattie, 2009, 2012); it also accelerates the practice of individual teachers while also affecting the level of collective teacher efficacy. The goal of microteaching is similar to that of instructional rounds. Its beauty is in its use of video.

Jim Knight (2014) advocates for the use of video as a powerful tool to improve professional learning. "When we record ourselves doing our work," he writes, "we see that reality is very different from what we think" (p. 2). We're sometimes disappointed by what we see, but often we're delighted. Either way, video helps us capture teacher and student behaviors that we might otherwise overlook. Teachers can use video individually to improve their practice, but it's most powerful when used with a colleague and when dialogue and feedback accompany it.

When leaders use collaboration to bridge the gap between high- and low-impact teachers, everybody wins. The leaders at Pixar Studios promote win-win interactions and a collaborative culture among their employees by teaching their people

- To listen, not talk.
- To practice empathy.
- To be comfortable with feedback.
- To lead and follow.
- To speak with clarity and avoid abstractions.
- To have win-win interactions.

Pixar made the shift to a learning culture when the leaders in the corporation realized that teams needed certain skills to be successful (Gino, 2019).

Now that we have organized our teams and laid the foundation for a collaborative protocol, it's time to experience the Achievement Teams four-step protocol.

## Key Takeaways

- The feedback cycle within Achievement Teams is all about creating a culture where educators use best practices and learn from what didn't work. Feedback is not about pointing fingers, but about professional growth.
- Giving and receiving feedback are crucial facets of Achievement Teams. By creating a culture based on collective efficacy, the feedback focuses on improving instruction and student results, not on personal feelings.
- Leaders can use feedback to coach teachers, with a focus on professional growth.
- Microteaching is a useful strategy for all team members to reflect on and learn from.

# 5

# Step 1: Collect and Chart the Data

*It's not about the numbers; it's about the*
*conversation that occurs as a result of the numbers.*

—John Hattie

Achievement Teams are about collectively searching for best practices using actual data on your students—and those data are a reflection of your impact. Working closely with John Hattie has taught us quite a lot about "knowing thy impact." For example, we acknowledge that data are essential because they drive change and provide a starting point for instruction. However, Hattie has made us aware that data only make a difference when teachers use them to assess their instructional impact. More to the point, if the data we collect don't challenge us, they don't change us.

In other words, looking at assessment results is not just about evaluating students and the progress they're making. It's about changing what we're doing as educators to help students reach their goals. If we have aligned an assessment appropriately with a specific learning target and the results are subpar, we don't change the assessment—we change the instruction.

The Achievement Teams framework is a four-step structured protocol that focuses on student achievement and teacher growth and promotes goal attainment for teachers and students. In Step 1, teams collect, organize, and chart the quantitative data to build a strong foundation for the remaining three steps. Our video, available at www.steveventura.com/achievement-teams/  videos.php or via the QR code on this page, introduces this step in detail. Figure 5.1 provides an overview of data use in this approach.

Achievement Teams focus on evidence from quality short-cycle assessments and use performance categories on those assessments to determine RTI strategies. Many student information systems in schools and districts provide access to online assessments, reports, and analyses. These systems often contain item banks of many high-quality standards-based assessments from which teachers can choose to build their custom assessments. This is all good news for busy teachers who need to administer, score, and analyze student assessment results within a short turnaround time.

**FIGURE 5.1**   Step 1: Collect and Chart the Data

**Key Points**
- ✓ Data help us decide on student groupings.
- ✓ Data can assist with instructional decisions.
- ✓ Data provide specific feedback to teachers and students.

**Application**
- ✓ Formative assessment helps us determine instructional next steps.
- ✓ Formative assessment helps us improve teaching and learning.
- ✓ Formative assessment helps us tailor lessons and instruction to student needs.

**Rationale**
- ✓ Data drive the actions of teachers and students in a learner-centered classroom.
- ✓ Data promote both teacher and student ownership of assessment results.

To assist with data collection, we have created a spreadsheet designed explicitly for Achievement Teams, which team members can use for both the pre- and post-assessment meetings. Just use the QR code on this page to access it, or go to www.steveventura.com/achievement-teams/resources-from-the-book.php. We created this resource to accurately reflect and communicate specific information about teachers and their students. Visual representation is an essential piece. The spreadsheet contains several key features; teachers can enter  assessment results, goals, and instructional strategies. More specifically, it includes pre- and post-assessment results by teacher groups and by individual teachers; a learning progressions planner; verbs associated with Webb's Depth of Knowledge, from simple to more complex; baseline evidence statements; and the high-impact instructional strategies teachers chose to address students' gaps in learning. In fact, all four steps of the Achievement Teams protocol are incorporated into this resource to make meetings more organized, efficient, and results oriented. Creating an accurate record of results means decisions are more thoughtful and data are more beneficial.

As a reminder, formative assessment results

- Inform the practice of teachers.
- Promote equity for all students.
- Build the capacity of all team members.
- Provide an effective strategy to determine if students have achieved the learning targets.
- Offer a powerful tool to appropriate new knowledge about teaching and learning.

Data collection from Achievement Teams' formative assessments does not need to be cumbersome and complicated. Figure 5.2 provides a basic template you can use to gather pre- and post-assessment data on a given learning target. Assessment results should be easily accessible, simple to understand, and, most important, organized so teachers can have purposeful conversations about teaching and learning.

## Step 1 in Action

To demonstrate Step 1—collect and chart the data—let's start with an example. It features a 7th grade English language arts assessment cycle using results from a pre-assessment.

**1. Students are given a 10-question selected-response pre-assessment based on this learning target:**

> **Determine** two or more central ideas in a text, and **analyze** their development over the course of the text; provide an objective **summary** of the text.

Normally a learning target that asks students to analyze and summarize may not be suitable for a selected-response assessment format (otherwise known as multiple-choice). You would expect students to use constructed-response items instead.

> **Selected Response:** More commonly referred to as multiple-choice, these assessment items ask students to choose a response.

> **Constructed Response:** These assessment items require students to respond in writing, either filling in blanks or writing one paragraph or less (short constructed response) or multi-paragraph responses (extended constructed response).

**FIGURE 5.2**   Achievement Teams Data Collection Template

**Step 1:** Collect and chart the data (derived from either a mirrored or an aligned pre-/post-assessment).

**Learning Target:**

| Pre-Assessment Results | | | | |
|---|---|---|---|---|
| Assessment Date: | | | | |
| Teacher | Excelling (9–10) | Achieving (7–8) | Progressing (5–6) | Beginning (<5) | Total Students |
| | | | | | |
| | | | | | |
| | | | | | |
| | | | | | |
| | | | | | |
| Totals | | | | | |

**Achievement Team:**                    **Meeting Date:**

| Post-Assessment Results | | | | |
|---|---|---|---|---|
| Assessment Date: | | | | |
| Teacher | Excelling (9–10) | Achieving (7–8) | Progressing (5–6) | Beginning (<5) | Total Students |
| | | | | | |
| | | | | | |
| | | | | | |
| | | | | | |
| | | | | | |
| Totals | | | | | |

**Achievement Team:**                    **Meeting Date:**

We realize there are limitations when using multiple-choice items, but there are advantages as well. Multiple-choice assessments

- Are easier to score.
- Can be used across several levels of cognitive demand.
- Produce results that are more conducive to item analysis.
- Can test a wider range of material than constructed-response-type items. (Haladyna, 2012).

In this example, teachers are beginning a cycle, so there must be a balance between the type of assessment they're using and the amount of time they have to score and reflect on assessment results. If they construct their selected-response assessment items properly, they can still assess students' critical thinking skills. Questions can range from simple recall to those that assess more advanced skills and concepts.

**2. Before administering the assessment, the 7th grade team determines the raw cut scores for arranging student results:**

- Beginning: Fewer than 5 items correct
- Progressing: 5–6 items correct
- Achieving: 7–8 items correct
- Excelling: 9–10 items correct

Teachers use cut scores to place students into performance categories to determine their current level of achievement. We're starting with a simple set of indicators to differentiate student outcomes. Using our performance level descriptors, we can organize our cut scores into the table shown in Figure 5.3.

No assessment is perfect, and neither are selected cut scores. Raw scores are the number of problems the students answered correctly. They are not weighted and are used to determine the actual "true" score. To clarify, cut scores are based on the number of items, not points. We have seen wide ranges of variance between pre- and post-assessments, and many times these variances are difficult to explain. However, we can improve assessment reliability when we create a consistent learning environment—for example, by giving students the same amount of time to complete the assessment and ensuring the environment has limited distractions. Also, the length of the assessment will improve reliability. We recommend 6–10 items for each learning target, and short-cycle assessments should not assess more than 1–2 targets.

**FIGURE 5.3**   Cut Scores and Percentage of Items Correct

Results are based on a 10-question selected-response pre-assessment.

| Performance Level | Number of Items Correct | Percentage Correct |
|---|---|---|
| Excelling | 9–10 | 90–100 |
| Achieving | 7–8 | 70–89 |
| Progressing | 5–6 | 50–69 |
| Beginning | Fewer than 5 | 0–49 |

3. **Teachers use a mirrored assessment model to compare "apples to apples" assessment results.** When starting the Achievement Teams process, we recommend using mirrored assessments. If the two assessments are the same, then it's only necessary to create the post-assessment and give it as the pre-assessment. Remember, mirrored assessments

- Are comparable in order to measure student growth between a pre- and post-assessment cycle.
- Are mostly identical.
- Enable teachers to make accurate inferences based on a set of clearly identified assessment items.

Most important, this type of assessment is designed to identify specific student needs while measuring change over two points in time (see Figure 5.4).

4. **Teachers use a "pre-teach/reteach" assessment cycle where they introduce and teach the skills and concepts they will assess before administering the pre-assessment.** Step 1 (collect and chart the data) does not go deep into data analysis, a topic we will address in Step 3 (create baseline evidence statements). Step 1 gives team members an opportunity to organize assessment results, gauge the accuracy of the assessment, and determine students' levels of proficiency on the basis of agreed-on cut scores.

Even though our example is simple, it does provide a viable solution for organizing assessment results. It demonstrates three key factors:

**FIGURE 5.4**   Pre- and Post-Assessment Results Template

**Step 1.** Collect and chart the data (derived from either a mirrored or an aligned pre-/post-assessment).

**Achievement Team**: 7th Grade          **Meeting Date:** April 8

**Learning Target: Determine** two or more central ideas in a text and **analyze** their development over the course of the text; provide an objective **summary** of the text.

| Pre-Assessment Results | | | | |
| --- | --- | --- | --- | --- |
| Assessment Date: March 15 | | | | |
| Teacher | Excelling (9–10) | Achieving (7–8) | Progressing (5–6) | Beginning (<5) | Total Students |
| Lopez | 5 | 6 | 6 | 4 | 21 |
| Thompson | 0 | 3 | 10 | 9 | 22 |
| Ruiz | 0 | 4 | 7 | 10 | 21 |
| Chen | 6 | 6 | 7 | 4 | 23 |
| Jackson | 3 | 4 | 6 | 7 | 20 |
| **Totals** | 14 | 23 | 36 | 34 | 107 |

| Post-Assessment Results | | | | |
| --- | --- | --- | --- | --- |
| Assessment Date: March 30 | | | | |
| Teacher | Excelling (9–10) | Achieving (7–8) | Progressing (5–6) | Beginning (<5) | Total Students |
| Lopez | 6 | 10 | 5 | 0 | 21 |
| Thompson | 4 | 7 | 6 | 5 | 22 |
| Ruiz | 7 | 6 | 7 | 1 | 21 |
| Chen | 8 | 9 | 4 | 2 | 23 |
| Jackson | 5 | 10 | 3 | 2 | 20 |
| **Totals** | 30 | 42 | 25 | 10 | 107 |

1. The number of students assessed in each individual classroom and the number of students at each performance level
2. The combined total number of students assessed across all five classrooms
3. The combined number of students at each performance level

Figure 5.5 shows the data as organized in pie charts.

**FIGURE 5.5**    Achievement Teams Data Sample: Pie Charts

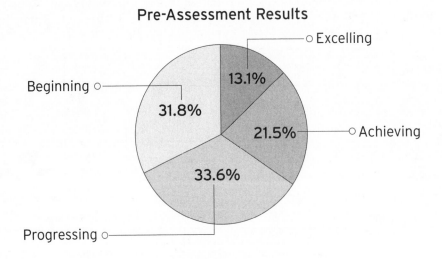

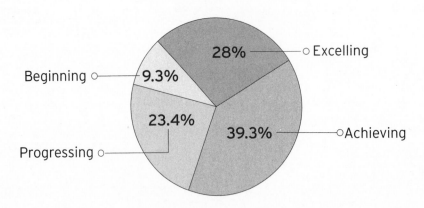

Step 1 ensures that assessment results are organized, accessible, and presented in a manner that is visually appealing. Collecting and charting data can help teachers make better-informed decisions. If you use the template shown in Figure 5.2 or something similar, make sure you organize your data using a consistent format, including frequency distributions that show how many of your students fall into the various performance categories.

## Success Criteria: Step 1

After teams have organized their assessment results, they can refer to the success criteria for Step 1, as shown in Figure 5.6.

**FIGURE 5.6** Success Criteria: Step 1

| | |
|---|---|
| ✓ | Results include the number of students at multiple performance levels (Excelling, Achieving, Progressing, Beginning). |
| ✓ | Results are organized in the Achievement Teams spreadsheet [see Figure 5.2] before the start of the meeting. |
| ✓ | Results include student work samples from the assessment. |
| ✓ | Results will provide specific feedback to students and teachers about skills and concepts that students achieved and those that students still need to learn. |

 The Leader's Role in Step 1

As Mike Schmoker (1999) points out, "Things get done only if the data we gather can inform and inspire those in a position to make a difference" (p. 77). Leadership involvement in Achievement Teams work is essential.

A few look-fors can help school leaders support teacher teams that complete Step 1:

*(continued)*

1. If teams are using an online database that stores and organizes assessment results, make sure all data are accessible to teachers and that the system is simple to use. These systems often produce reports based on a query. Selecting two or three report templates should suffice. It's sometimes overwhelming to navigate an online database. Make it easy for teachers to do so.

2. Teachers may not share their administrators' enthusiasm for data. To encourage teachers to be better practitioners around assessment results, leaders can provide additional coaching about how to view data as a method of inquiry. They can help teachers uncover micro-trends and pay attention to outlier scores or results that are not consistent with the average.

Remember, Step 1 results are connected to the four focus questions shown in Figure 5.7.

**FIGURE 5.7**  Achievement Teams Focus Questions

What strengths and gaps do the assessment results show?

What skills (verbs) and concepts (nouns and noun phrases) did students achieve regarding the learning target, and what do they still need to learn?

Who did we teach effectively, and who still needs help?

Which strategies did students use effectively? Which ones did they have trouble with?

**REFLECTION ACTIVITY**

Achievement Teams Focus Questions

Think about which of these four questions are a part of your collaborative protocol. Which questions would you consider adding to deepen the meeting? How will incorporating them into your team's conversation benefit both teachers and students?

## Key Takeaways

- The Achievement Teams framework is a four-step structured protocol that focuses the discussion on student achievement, teacher growth, and teacher effect to promote goal attainment for both teachers and students.
- Step 1 uses data from short-cycle assessments to provide specific feedback to students and teachers about skills and concepts that students did and did not achieve.
- Focus questions should guide your Achievement Teams meetings and conversations.

# 6

# Step 2: Set SMART Goals

*Setting goals is the first step in turning the invisible into the visible.*

—Anthony Robbins

Now that teams have organized assessment results and made initial observations, it's time to use this information to create relevant and meaningful goals. Goal setting helps the team determine the growth they want students to accomplish between the pre- and post-assessment, and it commits teachers to attaining that goal. Unfortunately, many schools don't keep track of the goals they have created and achieved, and others may not have achieved their goals in the first place.

This points to the importance of setting short-term goals—they lead to long-term success. Goals set over shorter periods of time motivate and create focus, and they increase the possibility of achieving the goal. In this chapter, you'll learn how to create Achievement Team goals for students and teachers, and you'll understand the benefits of both.

## Start with SMART Goals

Creating goals has a tremendous effect on academic outcomes. "Goals have a self-energizing effect if they are appropriately challenging for the student, as they can motivate students to exert effort in line with the difficulty or demands of the goal," explains Hattie (2009, p. 164). Achievement Teams replicate the same sense of motivation when harnessing teachers' instructional efforts toward a common goal (see Figure 6.1). Our brief video, available at www. steveventura.com/achievement-teams/videos.php or via the QR code on this page, introduces this step in more detail.

Let's begin by clarifying how we define SMART goals within the Achievement Teams framework. SMART goals are *learner* goals; in Achievement Teams, we use

SMART goals to create a growth target between the pre- and post-assessment. Achievement Teams follow the goal framework formulated by George T. Doran (1981), which stipulates that goals should be

- Specific,
- Measurable,
- Achievable,
- Relevant, and
- Time-bound.

**FIGURE 6.1**  Step 2: Establish SMART Goals

**Key Points**
- ✓ Goal setting motivates both teachers and students to exert extra effort in line with a specific task.
- ✓ Goal setting must be explicitly taught to students.
- ✓ Students perform better when they set their own goals, as opposed to having goals created for them.

**Application**
- ✓ Goal setting is used to determine a growth target between a pre- and post-assessment.
- ✓ Goals have a greater effect when they are written at an appropriate level of challenge.
- ✓ Goals are set for both teachers and students.

**Rationale**
- ✓ Goal setting is a metacognitive process that helps both teachers and students modify their learning behaviors.
- ✓ Teachers and students who create goals perform better than those who do not have goals.

# Three Methods of Goal Setting

Now that the team has administered the pre-assessment and organized the results, it's time to set a goal before administering the post-assessment. To maximize their impact, be sure to share goals with students.

We encourage teams to consider setting goals using one of the three methods that follow.

## Method 1. Grade- or Content-Level Goals

Here, a group of teachers sets a goal for their collective students. This goal is a formal part of Achievement Teams. Let's go back for a moment and review our pre-assessment results, as shown in Figure 6.2.

**FIGURE 6.2**   Learning Target Teacher Chart

**Focus Learning Target: Determine** two or more central ideas in a text and **analyze** their development over the course of the text; provide an objective **summary** of the text.

| Teachers | Excelling at Learning Intention (9–10 correct) | Achieving Learning Intention (7–8 correct) | Progressing Toward Learning Intention (5–6 correct) | Beginning Understanding of Learning Intention (<5 correct) | Total Students |
|---|---|---|---|---|---|
| Lopez | 5 | 6 | 6 | 5 | 22 |
| Thompson | 0 | 3 | 10 | 9 | 22 |
| Solorio | 0 | 4 | 7 | 10 | 21 |
| Rodriguez | 6 | 6 | 7 | 4 | 23 |
| Hayes | 3 | 4 | 6 | 7 | 20 |
| **Totals** | **14** | **23** | 36 | 35 | 108 |

Now that the team has organized the results, it's time to set an overall SMART goal. You will notice that Figure 6.2 has highlighted the number of students in the Excelling and Achieving categories. We combine these two totals to determine our current level of proficiency after the pre-assessment; we find that 37 students are proficient on the pre-assessment.

There is a total of 108 students across all five classrooms. Therefore, our current percentage of proficient students is 37/108, or 34 percent. Now the team decides on a goal to achieve after the post-assessment. They realize that 36 students are Progressing and another 35 students are Beginning, for a total of 71 students in those two areas.

One method to calculate a growth target is to have the team determine the total number of students from Progressing and Beginning who they think may score at least seven items correct on the post-assessment (the minimum number of items for a student to land in the Achieving category). This involves individual teachers looking at student scores and using their best professional judgment to determine the number of students in their class who might move up to the Achieving category, then combining that total with the respective totals from the rest of the team.

For example, let's suppose that after this exercise, the team determines that they can maintain the percentage of students who are already proficient (34 percent). This means that students who are already in the Excelling and Achieving categories will not revert to Progressing or Beginning. Then they determine the percentage of students from Progressing and Beginning who can potentially move to at least the Achieving category.

Of the 71 nonproficient students, the team believes 42 students can reach Achieving on the post-assessment. That would be 38 percent (42/108 = 38 percent). The team then adds 38 percent to the existing percentage of proficient students (34 percent) to determine the growth target: 38 + 34 = **72 percent**. For clarification, moving students from 34 to 72 percent would be considered substantial growth. Here's the goal they decided on:

> Our pre-assessment results revealed the students are struggling to determine two central ideas and summarize the text (they are 38 percent proficient). Our goal is that by the end of the pre-/post-assessment cycle, **at least** 72 percent of students will demonstrate understanding of both central ideas and summarizing the text, as verified through their writing.

**Progress and Growth.** We often work with schools and districts that create static goals, where the current level of student proficiency does not influence the selection of a specific target. This means that the target rarely changes. For example, the most common target we see schools select is 80 percent because it seems like a safe bet. This can be either too low or too high, depending on the baseline data.

We want to be clear about our goal-setting process. Some academic goals should be set at 95–100 percent mastery. For example, we would not want to set an 80 percent goal for those who deploy a parachute after leaping out of a plane. We would all prefer that our parachute opens 100 percent of the time. In education, academic goals should be set at 100 percent in the following instances:

- Good readers need to recognize letters 100 percent of the time.
- Students need to demonstrate number recognition and number order 100 percent of the time.

But consider our learning target:

> **Determine** two or more central ideas in a text and **analyze** their development over the course of the text; provide an objective **summary** of the text.

What appears to be a single learning target actually comprises five separate learning objectives, since students have to determine at least twice, analyze twice, and summarize once. This demonstrates how difficult it can be to reach mastery.

Achievement Team goals are a combination of growth and mastery goal setting. A growth goal takes into consideration the achievement levels of students at the beginning of an assessment cycle. They're more individual because they're based on the needs of each student. When students learn how to use effective learning strategies to reach their goals, they become intrinsically motivated to reach their growth target.

The purpose of an Achievement Teams cycle is to have as many students proficient as possible, but goal setting must be realistic. Many students from the Beginning level will likely move to at least Progressing, although this movement will not affect the proficiency needle.

Goals must be realistic, but we tend to aim high, creating appropriate levels of challenge while creating a staircase to mastery. Remember, teams can create and modify goals that represent the best collective thinking of the group.

Let's recap the entire SMART goal using our recently collected data:

> The percentage of students scoring in Achieving and higher using **informational text** will increase from **34 percent** to **72 percent** as measured by a team-created, formative short-cycle assessment administered on **April 29.**

One way to determine if your goal meets all of the SMART criteria is to make certain you have addressed all aspects of it:

**Specific:** We are focusing on a single learning target.
**Measurable:** We will calculate pre- and post-assessment results.
**Achievable:** Our goals are set at an appropriate level of challenge.
**Relevant:** Students struggle with this learning target. If they master it, they will enter the next grade level with confidence and a readiness to learn.

**Timely:** We have set a date to determine progress and growth.

To improve decision making in the entire building, many Achievement Teams schools incorporate data walls that provide schoolwide discussion around improving student achievement. Data walls or other similar exhibits contain relevant and timely information around instructional strategies and assessment results, and they provide shared opportunities to celebrate success and make clear inferences and conclusions.

## Method 2. Classroom Goals for Each Class

Publicly sharing individual student scores is not the best practice when creating a classroom data wall. Not only could we be shaming some students, but we also may be violating student privacy laws. Many teachers have said that their data walls include individual student scores or proficiency levels, but instead of indicating the student's name, they use a number or another code in place of it. Despite these well-intentioned efforts, the students typically see through the "codes." However, other research indicates that data walls can motivate students, especially higher-performing students at the middle school level, because of the sense of competition between classrooms.

If teachers elect to display assessment results publicly, whole-group goals that use the number of students but don't include specific student names or codes may provide class motivation. Tammy Heflebower and colleagues (Heflebower, Hoegh, Warrick, & Flygare, 2019) have created some helpful guidelines demonstrating the differences between comparison orientation goals and mastery orientation goals (see Figure 6.3). As you can see, mastery orientation goals are more focused on student growth and student analysis, and individual students or the teacher can chart their results privately.

Figure 6.4 shows how a teacher might use group goals to motivate students as a whole class. Seven common formative assessments (CFAs) are listed. The percentage of students who are proficient and above on a given pre-assessment appears on the left side of the table, and the percentage of students proficient or above on the post-assessment appears on the right side. For example, on the first common formative assessment administered, 46 percent of students were proficient or above, whereas 68 percent were proficient or above on the post-assessment. By posting the results on the board for the class to see, the teacher can convey a message of growth and progress.

**FIGURE 6.3**   Comparison Orientation Goals and Mastery Orientation Goals

| Teacher Behaviors That Reflect a Comparison Orientation | Teacher Behaviors That Reflect a Mastery Orientation |
|---|---|
| The teacher | The teacher |
| 1. Publicly shares group-level data or individual results in the belief that social comparison motivates students. | 1. Helps students identify weaknesses, ways to address gaps in learning, and so on. |
| | 2. Focuses on growth-related feedback by showing a clear relationship between effort and outcomes. |
| 2. Uses extrinsic rewards like prizes and parties when students move to a certain proficiency status. | 3. Encourages students to chart their results. |
| | 4. Shares individual-level results privately with students. |
| 3. Provides limited opportunities for student involvement; simply shares results. | 5. Focuses attention on how students perform in relation to their past performances. |
| | 6. Sometimes uses tangible rewards like praise and discussion or results toward progress. |
| 4. Provides little guidance about what students should study or revisit. | 7. Involves students in analysis, goal setting, and follow-up. |
| | 8. Uses whole-group or individual interventions and multiple approaches for reteaching. |

*Source:* From *A Teacher's Guide to Standards-Based Learning* (p. 49) by T. Heflebower, J. K. Hoegh, P. B. Warrick, & J. Flygare. © 2019 by Marzano Resources. Adapted with permission.

## Method 3. Personal Goal Setting for Students

Students' personal goals must include an appropriate level of challenge and clearly identify gaps in learning. According to the Visible Learning research (Hattie, 2012), teachers can maximize this process if they show students how to write their own goals. Teachers can conduct one-to-one goal-setting conferences with students to help them create goals that represent the correct level of difficulty. Here, we're focusing on goals between pre- and post-assessment results. Goals that include specific performance scores or targets are more likely to motivate students than general admonitions like "do your best."

Contrary to what some may believe, we can teach younger students to create and understand a learning goal and celebrate growth whether they achieve the goal or not. The most crucial factor in student goal setting is for teachers to be explicit in their goal-setting instructions. The more detailed the explanation, the better students will grasp the process and understand how to use it to increase their achievement level.

One strategy to accomplish this is to use a student self-reflection form:

- Students are given the total points possible from the assessment, and they record their current pre-assessment results on the form.
- The teacher asks them to set a goal before the second assessment takes place. Students conference with their teacher to determine the steps they will take to achieve their goal.
- Students record their actual assessment results from the post-assessment and fill out a self-reflection questionnaire.

**FIGURE 6.4**  Big Picture Reporting: Class Goals

| Learning Target | Pre-Assessment | Post-Assessment |
|---|---|---|
| CFA #1<br>Solve two-step word problems using the four operations. | 46% | 68% |
| CFA #2<br>Use multiplication and division within 100 to solve word problems. | 32% | 71% |
| CFA #3<br>Determine the unknown whole number in a multiplication equation relating three whole numbers. | 63% | 84% |
| CFA #4<br>Multiply and divide within 100 using correct properties of operations. | 58% | 72% |
| CFA #5<br>Use place-value understanding to round whole numbers to the nearest 10 or 100. | 40% | 75% |
| CFA #6<br>Compare two fractions with the same numerator or the same denominator by reasoning about their size. | 51% | 73% |
| CFA #7<br>Partition shapes into parts with equal areas. | 48% | |

Figure 6.5 shows an example of how students can set their own goals during the Achievement Teams short-cycle assessment framework. The teacher sets the target at 7 because that's how many answers students need to get correct to land in the Achieving category. Note that on the actual student form, this expectation would not be in boldface; we have illustrated it in the chart for reference. This goal may be discussed during the goal-setting meeting between the student and teacher.

**FIGURE 6.5**    Sample Student Self-Reflection Tool for Goal Setting

| | | | |
|---|---|---|---|
| 10 | Excelling 9–10 items correct | | | Target: at least 7 correct |
| 9 | | | 9 correct Excelling | |
| 8 | Achieving 7–8 items correct | | | 7 correct Achieving |
| 7 | | | | |
| 6 | Progressing 5–6 items correct | | | |
| 5 | | | | |
| 4 | Beginning 0–4 items correct | 4 correct Beginning | | |
| 3 | | | | |
| 2 | | | | |
| 1 | | | | |
| | Number of Items/ Cut Scores/ Proficiency Levels | Individual Student Pre-Assessment Score | Student-Created Goal | Individual Student Post-Assessment Score |

Before giving the pre-assessment, Achievement Team members set the cut scores to determine the Beginning, Progressing, Achieving, and Excelling levels. The graph shown in Figure 6.5 is based on a 10-question assessment, and the cut scores are listed in the first column on the left-hand side.

**Step 1. Students enter a pre-assessment score.** Students record their pre-assessment results in the second column on the graph. In this sample, the student scored a 4. Along with their results, teachers provide the students with accurate and timely feedback to help them understand their progress.

**Step 2. Students select a personal goal.** After teacher modeling and discussion around SMART goals, students predict how many more questions they believe they can score correctly on the post-assessment. They record this in the third column; you can see that this student has selected a score of 9. To assist with this process, you may consider adding a suggested target to the self-reflection tool. In our example, we're proposing a minimum of seven items correct, which essentially means minimum proficiency. If you do suggest a target, do so with care.

**Step 3. Students enter a post-assessment score.** Once you score and share the post-assessment results with students, they can enter their score in the last column and begin the self-reflection process. In this model, students create an engaging visual that permits them to look at their progress throughout the pre- and post-assessment cycle.

We're often asked what happens if students are already excelling on the pre-assessment. Should they even take the post-assessment? When we consider pre-assessment results with an unusually high level of success, we usually come to one of two conclusions:

1. Students were assessed on the content they mastered, and their success is a result of excellent teaching.

2. Students were assessed on content that may not have been set at the correct level of cognitive demand, and the assessment items need to be calibrated.

The teacher team would need to discuss these two scenarios to accurately infer causes for high and low scores. Requiring a student who has demonstrated mastery of the pre-assessment to take the post-assessment depends on what the team is most interested in learning. For example,

1. If the teacher is confident that the student demonstrates mastery on the pre-assessment, then the student may not be required to take the post-assessment, but this will skew the data. We can only compare students who took both assessments.

2. On occasion, we have seen students score higher on the pre- than on the post-assessment. This could be caused by a change in student motivation, an inconsistency between the two assessments, or another factor unrelated to teaching and learning. This may be a reason for students to take both assessments.

**Calculating Learning Gain Scores.** For those thrill seekers who would like to go deeper in analyzing goals between pre- and post-assessment, we recommend calculating the learning gain scores for each individual student. Typically, students score higher on the post-assessment, and there's a way to quantify this information.

Figure 6.6 shows the formula for positive gain using our student self-reflection tool for goal setting. The student in question answered 4 of 10 questions correctly on the pre-assessment (40 percent) and 7 of 10 questions correctly on the post-assessment (70 percent).

**FIGURE 6.6**   Calculating Learning Gain

Formula for positive gain (i.e., when an individual student scores higher on their post-test than on their pre-test):

$$\frac{(\text{Post-assessment} - \text{Pre-assessment})}{100\% - \text{Pre-assessment}}$$

Post-assessment is the **percentage correct** on the post-unit assessment
Pre-assessment is the **percentage correct** on the pre-unit assessment

Example for our student:    $\dfrac{70 - 40}{100 - 40} = \dfrac{30}{60} = 0.50$

This student demonstrated a gain of 30 percentage points out of a potential 60 percentage points they could have gained. Therefore, this student gained 0.50 (or 50%) of the possible percentage points they could have gained from the pre- to post-assessment.

*Source:* Formula from "Interactive-Engagement Versus Traditional Methods: A Six-Thousand-Student Survey of Mechanics Test Data for Introductory Physics Courses," by R. Hake, 1998, *American Journal of Physics, 66*(1), pp. 64–74.

**Student Aspirations and Goal Setting.** It's not uncommon for students to choose a goal that is 100 percent or, as in this example, to select 9 as a target on the post-assessment. Depending on the student, this may or may not be a realistic goal. To be sure, we would never tell a student that their expectations are too high and that they should lower their goal. As L. E. Madden (1997) once said, "Goal setting is a target to aim for rather than a standard which must be reached" (p. 411).

However, it's concerning to see a student set an ambitious goal and then not attain it. This may cause discouragement. Students simply need to understand that they may not achieve their goals and that there's nothing wrong with this and that they can continue to create ambitious goals and try again. Alternatively, some students underestimate their potential and choose a goal that doesn't challenge them. In either scenario, teachers need to stress appropriate targets for students to aim for.

Teachers can use this activity for lower elementary, upper elementary, middle, and high school students. As opposed to assigned goals, self-set goals can lead to the highest levels of student self-efficacy and performance (Schunk, 1985).

With Achievement Teams, the time between pre- and post-assessments is about two to three weeks. Therefore, the goals we create in this instance are short-term goals, permitting students to stay motivated; in fact, we encourage students to review their goal every day. The goals are also more granular because the formative assessments used for Achievement Teams focus on one to two learning targets. We also believe that when students write their own goals, they heighten their commitment to achieving them.

After the students complete their assessment chart, they can move into self-reflection about their current results and performance. Here are some sample prompts for them to consider:

- What are some things I did well?
- What parts of the assessment were the easiest?
- One of the things I do best is...
- Some areas I need to improve in are...
- What parts of the assessment was I unsure about?
- I will need help with...
- The most challenging part of this assessment was...

## Success Criteria: Step 2

After teams have set goals based on assessment results, they can refer to the success criteria for Step 2, as shown in Figure 6.7.

Whatever method your team chooses to create, implement, and share goals, you now have a quantifiable resource to help track achievement. This process includes your students; be sure to encourage them to check and remind themselves of their own personal goals.

**FIGURE 6.7**   Success Criteria: Step 2

| | |
|---|---|
| ✓ | Goals are established based on students' current levels of proficiency using a growth formula or teacher professional judgment. |
| ✓ | SMART goals are shared with students. |
| ✓ | Students set individual goals between the pre- and post-assessment. |
| ✓ | Achievable gains in student learning take into account the current performance of all students and/or are based on the use of a growth formula. |
| ✓ | An agreed-on time is set for the administration of the post-assessment. |

 The Leader's Role in Step 2

For school leaders, there are a few look-fors that can provide support to teacher teams during Step 2:

  • Leaders should seek evidence to ensure that both large-scale goals (grade-level goals) and small-scale goals (students' individual goals) are part of the Achievement Teams process.
  • As a common practice, leaders should be able to discuss both individual and classroom goals with students. This is a great strategy for classroom walkthroughs to ensure that goals are a part of the learning process for all.

 **REFLECTION ACTIVITY**
Methods for Tracking Goals

Which method or methods do you believe your team will use to track goals during the Achievement Teams process? Why?

| |
|---|
| |

# Key Takeaways

- Step 2 uses the evidence from pre-assessment results to establish SMART goals for both teachers and students.
- Goal setting for both teachers and students has tremendous potential.
- Goals
  - Provide clarity while creating a destination.
  - Motivate, especially if they are appropriately challenging.
  - Encourage higher levels of performance and create a sense of satisfaction.
  - Provide opportunities for self-reflection, metacognitive learning, and greater overall success.

# 7

# Step 3: Create Baseline Evidence Statements

*I have no data yet. It is a capital mistake to theorize before one has data.*

—Sherlock Holmes, in *A Scandal in Bohemia* (Doyle, 1891)

Baseline evidence statements are summary statements derived from formative assessment results that help teachers make inferences about student performance levels. To arrive at the statements, teachers conduct root cause analysis based on the pre-assessment results. The rich, collaborative discussions that ensue promote the core purpose of Achievement Teams: to continually assess our impact as teachers and leaders. This step is designed to help teachers reflect on their practice while enabling them to determine effective instructional strategies between the pre- and post-assessment (see Figure 7.1). Our brief video, available at www.steveventura.com/achievement-teams/videos.php or via the QR code on this page, introduces this step in more detail.

As teams begin to examine evidence and reflect on instructional impact, it's important to revisit two mindframes from the Visible Learning research:

1. My fundamental task is to evaluate the effect of my teaching on students' learning and achievement.

2. All assessments, including formative assessments, are more a reflection of my effort than of my students' effort.

With these in mind, let's look again at our four focus questions, which teachers can also use in post-assessment conversations:

1. What strengths and gaps do the assessment results show?

2. What skills (verbs) and concepts (nouns and noun phrases) were achieved from the learning target, and what still needs to be learned?

3. Who did we teach effectively, and who still needs help?

4. Which instructional strategies were effective? Which ones were less effective?

We designed these prompts to help team members identify which teaching methods were effective and which ones they might improve. As team members have conversations during meetings, they can identify why certain strategies worked and others didn't, or if differences in teaching style and delivery affected the success of each strategy.

**FIGURE 7.1   Step 3: Create Baseline Evidence Statements**

**Key Points**
- ✓ Baseline evidence statements (cognitive strengths and needs) are within the direct influence of teachers.
- ✓ Baseline evidence statements promote collective efficacy.
- ✓ Baseline evidence statements help teachers evaluate the effect of their teaching.

**Application**
- ✓ Baseline evidence statements are the product of responding to four Achievement Team focus questions.
- ✓ Baseline evidence statements promote root cause analysis based on assessment results.

**Rationale**
- ✓ Teacher collaboration works best when team members identify what methods of teaching were effective and what they can improve.

# The Quality of the Conversation: Building Relationships

The core of Step 3 is centered on teacher dialogue within the Achievement Teams framework. For effective dialogue to occur, team members must have a foundation of trust and a culture grounded in collective efficacy. During this step, teachers need to embrace evidence-based conversation while collaboratively searching for a root cause of student learning. As indicated earlier, the bulk of the meeting time will take place in Steps 3 and 4.

Researchers Bryk and Schneider (2002) spent four years in 12 different Chicago school communities determining how the effects of relational trust influence school reform efforts. They developed a six-point teacher trust scale to assist schools and districts with ascertaining the level of trust that exists among colleagues (ranging from Strongly Disagree to Strongly Agree) with the following criteria:

- Teachers at this school trust one another.
- Teachers at this school feel comfortable discussing feelings, worries, and frustrations with other teachers.
- Teachers at this school respect other teachers who take the lead in improvement efforts.
- Teachers at this school respect other teachers who are experts at their craft.
- I feel respected by other teachers at this school. (Bryk & Schneider, 2002, p. 157)

What they discovered is that people can amplify relational trust through their social exchanges during collaboration. Even more notable were the regressive effects of an absence of trust, which resulted in schools having little or no chance of improving.

Feeling trusted and respected can actually improve school reform efforts. Bryk and Schneider found that schools with strong levels of trust at the outset of reforms had a 1-in-2 chance of making significant improvements in math and reading, whereas those with weak relationships had only a 1-in-7 chance of making gains.

Great relationships alone will not improve instruction, but schools that maintain high levels of relational trust are more likely to make instructional decisions that significantly improve student achievement than schools in which relationships are poor.

 **REFLECTION ACTIVITY**

Creating a Culture of Feedback

Creating a culture that accepts and acts on feedback is an important task for all team members. Here are two crucial learning mindframes:

> • I give and help students understand feedback, and I interpret and act on feedback given to me.
> • I build relationships and trust so learning can occur in a place where it's safe to make mistakes and learn from others.
>
> How can you create an environment where your team feels comfortable acting on feedback, implementing new strategies, and making mistakes?

## Root Cause Analysis

Root cause analysis is a structured team process that assists in identifying the factors and causes of an event. Understanding the contributing factors to or the direct causes of failure can help people develop actions that sustain corrections (SNFQAPI, 2019). Through Achievement Teams, teachers wisely identify all of the factors that cause a problem before attempting to solve it.

We have found that providing teachers with prompts and discussion points can accelerate their conversation and help them arrive at conclusions within the time they have to meet. Using short-cycle assessment data is about developing an awareness of what teachers need to improve. The results from the pre-assessment provide them with important information about their students' readiness to learn, as well as with opportunities to reteach the missing skills.

Here are additional prompts that teachers can consider as they analyze assessment results:

- What are the strengths of the student responses?
- What skills and concepts proved to be the most challenging for students?
- Which questions had the highest number of correct responses? (This could indicate great teaching or an easy assessment.)
- Which questions had the lowest number of correct responses? (These questions will assist with targeted instruction.)
- Which questions had a low response or no response at all? (These questions will assist with targeted instruction.)

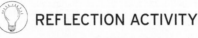

**REFLECTION ACTIVITY**

Assessment Prompts

How have you used similar prompts in the past to reflect on student out-comes? Which prompts did you use? What other ways do you address assessment results in terms of teaching practice? For example, you may ask which items on the assessment had the highest number of correct responses or, by contrast, which items had the lowest number of correct responses.

## Sample Baseline Evidence Statements

Figure 7.2 summarizes what teachers learned from a pre-assessment of the learning target, *Determine two or more ideas in a text and analyze their development over the course of the text; provide an objective summary of the text.* The teachers included evidence for each focus question.

The first two questions listed in the figure deal with assessment strengths and gaps, with what students did and didn't learn. For example, some students were able to analyze the central ideas in the text, but others had difficulty determining at least two central ideas. The third focus question deals with the percentage of students who did and didn't achieve the learning target. In this case, although 35 percent of the assessed students demonstrated understanding of the target, 65 percent had difficulty determining the main idea or explaining how key details supported that idea. The fourth and final focus question deals with which strategies were and weren't effective. The teachers found that collaborative partner work and close reading strategies worked far better than having students fill out worksheets.

**FIGURE 7.2**    Sample Baseline Evidence Statements

**Step 3:** Create baseline evidence statements.

**What are baseline evidence statements?** They are statements that summarize the evidence that teams have gathered from the administration of a short-cycle pre-assessment. Teams can create their evidence statements by responding to four Achievement Teams focus questions.

| FOCUS QUESTIONS | SUMMARY OF EVIDENCE | |
|---|---|---|
| | **Learning Target: Determine** two or more ideas in a text and **analyze** their development over the course of the text; provide an objective **summary** of the text. | |
| **What strengths and gaps do the assessment results show?** | **Assessment Result Strengths**<br>• Students can look at the order in which evidence is presented when they describe how a main idea is developed over the course of a text.<br>• Students can analyze the development of central ideas and communicate their analysis in an unbiased summary of the text. | **Gaps**<br>• Some students had difficulty with determining at least two central ideas of a text.<br>• Some struggled with writing objective summaries of a text. |
| **What skills (verbs) and concepts (nouns and noun phrases) did students achieve regarding the learning target, and what do they still need to learn?** | **Skills and Concepts Achieved**<br>• Students identified two or more central ideas over the course of a full text.<br>• Students were able to provide quality responses to support their main point. | **Needs to Be Achieved**<br>• Some students were only able to identify a single central idea and use details to explore how it was conveyed.<br>• Some students struggled with determining the central idea of a text and how it was conveyed through specific details. |
| **Who did we teach effectively, and who still needs help?** | **Students Achieving**<br>• About **35%** of the students assessed demonstrated understanding of this learning target. | **Students Not Achieving**<br>• But **65%** of the students could not determine the main idea, explain how it was supported by key details, and summarize the text. They could perform some but not all of the details required to achieve this learning target. |

*(continued)*

FIGURE 7.2    Sample Baseline Evidence Statements—(*continued*)

| FOCUS QUESTIONS | SUMMARY OF EVIDENCE | |
|---|---|---|
| | **Learning Target: Determine** two or more ideas in a text and **analyze** their development over the course of the text; provide an objective **summary** of the text. | |
| **Which strategies did students use effectively? Which ones did they have trouble with?** | **Effective Strategies**<br>• Collaborative partner work<br>• Close reading/modeling<br>• Jigsaw method<br>• Use of success criteria | **Less Effective Strategies**<br>• Worksheets<br>• Instruction emphasized too much surface-level learning and did not include deep-level learning. |

## The Fishbone Diagram

Several tools can help users identify possible causes of an effect and specific root problems. The fishbone diagram is a cause-and-effect tool created by organizational theorist and engineer Kaoru Ishikawa (1989) that teams can use when they get stuck around baseline evidence statements or struggle to articulate root causes. Users place the impact or results in the head of the fish and then list potential reasons that preceded that effect on the bones of the fish.

In the fishbone diagram shown in Figure 7.3, the teachers considered why students had difficulty determining two central ideas in a text. They found that students struggled with citing quotes in support of an idea. Also, on the instructional end, they believed there may have been limited focus on how text structures help readers identify the main idea.

As we look at this process as a whole, we recommend a pre-teach/reteach assessment model for several reasons. In this cycle, we treat the first set of assessment results as a first draft; this enables both teachers and students to make essential adjustments. It's OK to acknowledge that teachers and students may not do their best work on the first assessment.

The Foreword to this book mentioned Bob Stake's soup analogy. When chefs taste their soup, they have the opportunity to improve the flavor, adjust the temperature, and make sure it's ready to serve. This is the same philosophy for incorporating a pre-teach/reteach assessment cycle—because when the guest tastes the soup (a summative assessment), the opportunity to improve the flavor may no longer be available.

**FIGURE 7.3**  Fishbone Diagram

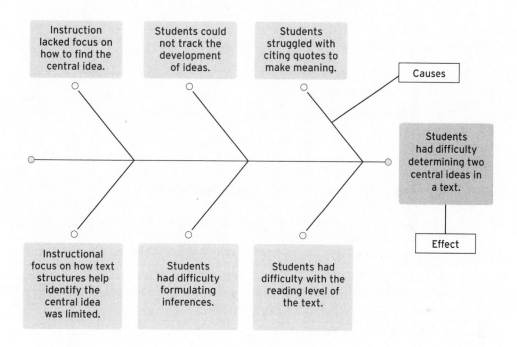

In this example, teachers determined that
students could not identify central ideas within a text.

## Measuring Our Success

Data analysis can be extremely dynamic, meaning that the results of the assessment provide teachers with real-time evidence while reducing toxic conversations, such as blaming students for their inability to demonstrate proficiency. Blaming requires no particular skill, but working collectively to seek solutions builds a strong team that can turn evidence into action.

Assessment results permit teachers to look for and learn from outliers, those students who score well above or below the average of the class. Imagine how rich our conversations would be if we could identify what preceded a given set of results, replicate what worked, and discontinue what didn't. This is the true spirit of creating baseline evidence statements; they're an honest evaluation of educators' impact.

## Success Criteria: Step 3

After teams have created baseline evidence statements, they can refer to the success criteria for Step 3, as shown in Figure 7.4.

**FIGURE 7.4**   Success Criteria: Step 3

| | |
|---|---|
| ✓ | Teams make inferences regarding student progress by analyzing pre-assessment results. |
| ✓ | The evidence statements and needs identified are within the direct influence of teachers. |
| ✓ | Conversations are purposeful and are based on the four Achievement Teams focus questions:<br>• What strengths and gaps do the assessment results show?<br>• What skills (verbs) and concepts (nouns and noun phrases) were achieved from the learning target, and what still needs to be learned?<br>• Who did we teach effectively, and who still needs help?<br>• Which instructional strategies were effective? Which ones were less effective? |
| ✓ | Teams identify root causes based on where students are in the learning progressions and on the pre-assessment results. |

 The Leader's Role in Step 3

It's crucial for Achievement Teams to create a climate of mutual respect and interdependence. Leaders can promote feedback and trust by listening intently during collaboration (see Figure 7.5). It's not enough to just sit at the same table with a team and observe their collaboration. Leadership posture communicates an important message—that you're positioning yourself to be a resource to Achievement Team members.

**FIGURE 7.5**   Promoting a Culture of Respect

| What | How |
| --- | --- |
| Good leaders *listen*.... | With purposeful intention. |
| Good leaders *ask*... | Questions for clarification. |
| Good leaders *contribute*... | When the team needs guidance and/or support. |
| Good leaders *disconnect*... | From personal devices. |

## Key Takeaways

- During Step 3, team members use four focus questions or conversation prompts to make inferences about the methods of teaching that proved most effective and what they can improve before the post-assessment.
- Teacher discussion and collaboration drive Step 3.
- Baseline evidence statements and the assessment process enable teachers to reflect on their practice before selecting the high-impact instructional strategies that work best.

# 8

# Step 4: Select High-Yield Instructional Strategies

*Planning instruction involves a paradox. On the one hand, teachers need to make deliberate plans that lay out exactly what will be learned. On the other hand, teachers need to be ready to adjust their plan when opportunity or slow progress suggests they need to change.*

—Jim Knight (2012)

Let's begin by defining what we mean by instructional strategies: *Instructional strategies are teacher actions designed to raise student levels of thinking and learning around specific learning targets. They are purposeful methods of instruction that help create vibrant, independent students who can assess their own learning.* With Achievement Teams, teachers can improve their practices and their classroom environment while putting in place a structured approach to addressing *all* student needs.

## Selecting Strategies That Meet Student Needs

During this step in the meeting cycle, teams select high-impact strategies that are targeted to student needs to advance learning. Teachers implement the strategies deliberately and practice them with fidelity with a view toward closing achievement gaps (see Figure 8.1). Our brief video, available at www.steveventura.com/achievement-teams/videos.php or via the QR code on this page, introduces this step in more detail.

Now that teams have pre-taught and pre-assessed their lesson, analyzed the assessment results, set goals, and determined the baseline evidence statements, it's time to select the corrective instructional strategies to implement before the post-assessment. The key to this step is to purposefully align instructional strategies to the pre-assessment results.

**FIGURE 8.1**   Step 4: Select High-Yield Instructional Strategies

**Key Points**
- ✓ Instruction is purposefully aligned to the pre-assessment results.
- ✓ Instructional strategies are designed to considerably accelerate student progress between pre- and post-assessments.

**Application**
- ✓ Teams review baseline evidence statements to determine student strengths and misconceptions.
- ✓ Instructional planning between pre- and post-assessments should be considered a fresh start, as opposed to just reteaching using the same lesson plans as before.

**Rationale**
- ✓ Instructional strategies directly target the strengths and gaps identified during Step 3: Create baseline evidence statements.
- ✓ Instructional strategies develop a course of action to address and solve instructional problems, creating additional opportunities for students to succeed.

Teachers now need to address student misunderstandings and misconceptions. To foster better strategy selection, team members review their responses to the Achievement Teams focus questions that we looked at in Step 3:

1. What strengths and gaps do the assessment results show?
2. What skills (verbs) and concepts (nouns and noun phrases) were achieved from the learning target, and what still needs to be learned?
3. Who did we teach effectively, and who still needs help?
4. Which instructional strategies were effective? Which ones were less effective?

Because the team collected these results early on in the teaching cycle, they have a fairly good idea of where to start and what skill level students need to achieve. They can now approach instructional planning between the pre- and post-assessment as a new beginning.

The instructional strategies selected should target the assessed skill level. This is where collaboration among the team is important. Members can share highly effective strategies that have worked for them in the past, or the team as a whole might decide to try a new strategy based on what they learned from the pre-assessment.

During this step, teachers can refer back to the learning progressions they created for the learning target. The learning progressions and the results of the pre-assessment will provide a roadmap for differentiation. Teachers can target strategies to a student's level on the progression. By doing so, they can provide challenging instructional strategies for those students who scored at the Excelling level and supporting strategies for those students who are not yet proficient. Teachers reflect as a team when a chosen strategy doesn't meet their expectations by reviewing assessment results. They may do an item analysis and determine which assessment items had the highest number of correct responses and which had the lowest number of correct responses and backward-map to the antecedents or strategies that were used for those items. When they identify which strategies resulted in the lowest gains, they can try a new approach that holds more promise.

## Choosing Instructional Strategies for Our Sample Learning Target

Let's look once again at our learning target:

> Determine two or more central ideas in a text and analyze their development over the course of the text; provide an objective summary of the text.

The most important part of this step is applying corrective instruction. Three skills are embedded within this single target. We'll now consider some options for each skill:

1. **Determine** <u>two or more central ideas in a text.</u>
2. **Analyze** <u>their development over the course of the text.</u>
3. **Summarize** <u>the text.</u>

### Determine Central Ideas

When it comes to determining central ideas, one of the most effective strategies we have seen is annotating text using a colored pencil or highlighter. Teachers need to explain to students that the purpose of annotating a given text is for readers to add helpful notes and information there about the topic under study. Even more effective is modeling for students how to accomplish this.

Students can circle, underline, bracket, or use different color highlighters. An annotation key can provide a visual for students to refer to as they complete this process. Figure 8.2 shows some of the more common symbols we have observed.

**FIGURE 8.2**  Determining the Central Ideas

| | |
|---|---|
| ———————————— | Main ideas and key details |
| (oval) | Unfamiliar words |
| ✳ | Important information |

Teachers can model how to use the three symbols shown in Figure 8.2—an underline, an oval, and an asterisk—using a short passage of a story or text. Teachers can also model how to use these techniques electronically. Most portable document formats (PDFs) are loaded with annotation tools, permitting students to use sticky notes, different-colored highlighters, text boxes, and basic shapes.

Students first need to understand a few things about central ideas. Central ideas (or main ideas)

- Help students understand what they're reading.
- Can usually be determined by referring to the heading of a text.
- Are typically written using general terms or topics; they usually don't contain explicit details.

From here, students can then use headings, subheadings, and other text features to assist them with this particular skill.

## Analyze the Development of Central Ideas

Start by providing students with a high-interest and engaging nonfiction article. Newsela (www.newsela.com) and Scholastic (www.scholastic.com) are great resources for articles in which authors argue their view on a topic while providing evidence and reasoning to back up their claims. Before the activity, begin by reviewing types of text features—such as titles, bold words, sidebars, labeled diagrams, and pictures and captions—and how they can help the reader understand the message the author is trying to convey.

Using the jigsaw method, divide students into "home" groups and assign each member of the group a different portion of the text. Let students know the purpose of this exercise: they will need to think critically as they analyze claims, reasons, and evidence in order to summarize information, make connections to the topic, share key points, and make inferences.

Have students silently read and annotate their section of the text. Next, have them move into "expert" groups with students who have the same section of text. Teachers may want to make discussion prompts available to the groups to facilitate deeper understanding. In their expert groups, students discuss their interpretation of the reading and prepare to share their understanding with their home group. Once back in their home groups, team members ask one another questions about how each member's particular section connects to the central idea of the text. At this point, have students read, analyze, and summarize the entire text.

## Summarize the Text

If students struggled with summarizing the text on the pre-assessment, a few strategies can help close this gap. First, explain that a summary is nothing more than a condensed version of whatever they're reading. The summaries should be *objective*; that is, students shouldn't interpret the text or include their personal feelings or reactions in their summaries. Teaching students to provide an objective summary of the text could begin with asking them to identify objective and non-objective statements. Such examples can guide students in writing statements and summaries that are void of their own personal feelings. Figure 8.3 shows several statements from a text about children and the value of playtime; have students read and classify the statements as either objective or nonobjective.

**FIGURE 8.3**  Objective Versus Nonobjective Statements

| Objective Statements | Nonobjective Statements |
| --- | --- |
| A 2019 study from the Ohio State University suggests that children need time to play during school. | Children probably don't learn when they're having fun. |
| When children play, they develop their social skills as they interact with others. | Students who don't get opportunities to play never turn in their assignments. |
| Playtime helps children understand the rules of the game and how to improve their skills. | The best playtime activities are football, soccer, and baseball. |

The next strategy might involve asking students to summarize a single paragraph from the text in one or two sentences, reminding them that they should use their own words and include objective statements. Figure 8.4 shows an example of a summary using the text about playtime. After this single-paragraph activity, students can summarize several paragraphs using this same technique. Finally, they can combine all their paragraph summaries into a single overall summary of the entire text.

**FIGURE 8.4**   Summary Example

When students play, they take time away from studies and reduce stress by exercising. Playtime can help students become better learners and can increase their focus when they are in their classrooms. The more students play, the better their physical fitness, leading to a healthier lifestyle.

Playtime can help students improve their fitness, reduce stress, and become better learners.

We strongly believe that success criteria and learning progressions contribute significantly to the effectiveness of instructional strategies and should be a part of high-functioning schools and districts. Clarity, combined with specific instructional strategies, permits teachers to extend their instructional influence while increasing student achievement.

## To Reteach or Not to Reteach?

Reteaching should be purposefully aligned to the pre-assessment results, not random choices of instruction. For reteaching to be effective, teachers must

- Use pre-assessment results as indicators.
- Create baseline evidence statements.
- Align instructional strategies to the strengths and gaps in the assessment results.
- Administer a post-assessment to determine instructional success.

**Reteaching cannot be a repeat.** Instruction between the pre- and post-assessment must respond to those gaps, mistakes, and misconceptions observed from the pre-assessment. This is an opportunity to create new learning that addresses specific errors. More important, when reteaching content that students struggle with, it's important *to not reteach it the way you originally taught it.*

Consider using these four prompts from Jim Knight (2012) to create your own instructional strategy playbook:

1. In one sentence, describe the strategy you have chosen to use.
2. What's the point? Clearly identify why you might use this strategy.
3. How might teachers use this strategy?
4. How might students use this strategy?

The following are sample responses to these four prompts drawing from the concept mapping strategy page in our own *Achievement Teams Instructional Strategy Flip Book* (Advanced Collaborative Solutions, 2020, p. 5):

1. Concept maps are an effective aid to processing and organizing information.
2. Concept mapping is a way of showing connections, making associations, and linking one idea to another. It is a great way to build and stretch the creative thinking of concrete sequential learners.
3. Teachers can use this strategy to help students see the connections between details and big ideas in any subject matter. Visualizing patterns and connecting abstract ideas allows students to reach higher levels of critical thinking.
4. This strategy is excellent for the student who learns best through visual or kinesthetic learning so that they can "draw" and see relationships between and among ideas.

## An Instructional Strategy Flip Book

To assist with instructional strategy selection, we have created the aforementioned digital flip book containing 25 instructional strategies. We selected these strategies on the basis of their effect on achievement and student progress. In the flip book, we describe each of the strategies, explain the rationale for using it, list the steps to implementing it, and discuss how both students and teachers will use it. Strategies include, among others, the following:

- Anchor activities
- Concept mapping
- Error analysis
- Exit cards
- Graphic organizers

- Jigsaw method
- Inquiry writing
- Numbered heads together
- Think-pair-share
- RAFT (role, audience, format, topic)
- Reciprocal teaching

The goal of this resource is to provide educators with examples of strategies that follow the four prompts noted above. You will note the relationship between the Visible Learning findings and strategy application. This flip book is available at www.steveventura.com/achievement-teams/resources-from-the-book.php or via the QR code on this page.

---

 **REFLECTION ACTIVITY**

Instructional Strategies

Which instructional strategies, either from the flip book or others you are familiar with, have you used in the past most successfully? How did you know these were successful?

---

Now that you've selected the appropriate strategies, it's time for implementation. Team members will incorporate these practices into their instruction before administering the post-assessment. Then they will determine if students have achieved the goals and if instruction had a positive effect.

## Surface, Deep, and Transfer Learning

In 2016, John Hattie and Gregory M. Donoghue published an article titled "Learning Strategies: A Synthesis and Conceptual Model" that introduced three phases of learning—surface, deep, and transfer—and shared a subset of strategies that have been proven effective via 228 meta-analyses. Hattie and Donoghue were looking at the effect size of different learning strategies. For example, the use of success criteria has a very high probability of accelerating student achievement. By contrast, homework at the elementary level has proven to be less effective.

In the model of learning they describe in their article, Hattie and Donoghue note that the three phases of learning can overlap and be accomplished simultaneously, especially surface and deep learning. Moreover, the authors stress that it may not be enough for students to acquire each phase of learning without consolidating that learning, meaning that students will be able to retrieve that information later.

When teams meet collaboratively and begin implementing instructional strategies, it may be beneficial to follow a model that addresses how strategies can be selected. The three phases of learning can help compartmentalize instruction that is meaningful to the student. Read on for a brief explanation of each phase and an activity in Figure 8.5 (pp. 117–123) to extend and apply your understanding. View a handout on surface, deep, and transfer learning at www.steveventura.com/achievement-teams/resources-from-the-book. php or via the QR code on this page.

## Surface Learning: Building Knowledge

Surface learning is factual learning, meaning that it is a prerequisite for deeper learning. In Achievement Teams, we encourage the use of learning progressions that contain prerequisite skills and concepts (surface) that lead to more advanced skills and concepts (deep). Therefore, surface learner strategies focus on recall or procedural information, like explaining, naming, note taking, and restating. Think of situations where your students are required to learn something new, like playing a musical instrument. Those initial music lessons are focused on reading music, playing scales, and learning rhythms (surface). Eventually, students can sight-read music, play entire passages, and perform for others (deep).

## Deep Learning: Making Meaning

Deep learning is a product of surface learning, where students can revisit and recall their surface-level knowledge and use it to obtain deeper learning. As Hattie explains, teachers tend to stay at the surface level of instruction. In fact, he proposes that 90 percent of instruction is designed to be at the surface level of learning. Therefore, deep learning connects to surface learning and combines them to progress to higher levels of achievement. Deep learning can be considered an extension of students' prior knowledge.

**FIGURE 8.5**  Surface, Deep, and Transfer Learning

An understanding of the three phases of learning can add tremendous value as teams discuss, research, and apply learning strategies. Even more important is a constant reminder of the types of instruction students currently receive. If Hattie believes that 90 percent of classroom instruction is surface learning, how can educators better select strategies that align with deep and transfer learning? How do teachers currently select instructional strategies as they examine and analyze assessment results?

The following table lists 17 strategies. Read the explanation of each strategy and determine which phase it best represents. Share a summary of that strategy and why you believe it is surface, deep, or transfer.

| Strategy | Explanation | Surface? Deep? Transfer? |
|---|---|---|
| **1. Organizing and Transforming Notes** | Transforming involves organizing information, but in this process, students rearrange information to show interrelationships between ideas. These interrelationships can include making comparisons, looking at cause-and-effect relationships, or identifying trends and patterns. The use of visuals while transforming notes can help the learner retain information more effectively. Examples of ways to transform information include Venn diagrams, concept maps, tables, graphs, and timelines. | |
| **2. Cooperative Learning** | Cooperative learning is a teaching strategy in which small groups of learners work together to accomplish a shared goal. This strategy allows students with different levels of ability to use their strengths to maximize learning for themselves and their group as a whole. Learners work together using higher-order thinking skills to solve complex problems. Team members use their skills to research, reflect, and apply prior knowledge to the given group assignment. Cooperative grouping creates a cohesive environment where members feel that they are a valuable part of their team, increasing motivation and achievement to accomplish a common goal. Studies have shown that when implemented correctly, cooperative learning leads to improved student attendance, behavior, achievement, and self-confidence in the classroom. | |

*(continued)*

**FIGURE 8.5**  Surface, Deep, and Transfer Learning—*(continued)*

| Strategy | Explanation | Surface? Deep? Transfer? |
|---|---|---|
| **3. Outlining** | Outlining is a strategy to organize thoughts or information related to a project or writing assignment. Using an outline at the beginning of the writing process helps to clarify thoughts and ideas in a structured hierarchy. Outlines demonstrate the thinking process behind a student's writing and provide teachers with a map to help guide further instruction. Students can use headings, subheadings, bulleted lists, and graphical techniques to separate main ideas from supporting details. | |
| **4. Massed Versus Spaced Practice** | Massed practice is a continuous task, usually completed in single long instructional sessions instead of frequent review. Spaced practice, which is presented in smaller chunks over time and includes rest time between intervals, permits students to retain information longer. Spaced practice contributes to long-term memory and learning retention. | |
| **5. Summarizing** | Summarizing teaches students to read a large selection of text and capture the most important ideas while excluding irrelevant or repetitive information. Summarization is an effective tool for improving students' memory and comprehension for reading and is effective for almost all content areas. Summarization must be explicitly taught and used frequently in order for students to become skilled in using this strategy. | |
| **6. Vocabulary Programs** | Vocabulary is the knowledge of words and their meanings. Having a rich vocabulary supports reading development and increases comprehension. Studies show a link between having a low vocabulary understanding and low reading comprehension scores, whereas students with a rich vocabulary have higher reading comprehension scores. The National Reading Panel (2000) recommended using a variety of indirect (incidental) and direct (intentional) methods of vocabulary instruction. Indirect vocabulary development comes | |

| Strategy | Explanation | Surface? Deep? Transfer? |
|---|---|---|
| **6. Vocabulary Programs—** (*continued*) | from being exposed to rich conversations and vocabulary at home and at school, both orally and in print. Students need targeted instruction in techniques for direct vocabulary development. Some research-based vocabulary learning strategies include using context clues, defining words in context, sketching words to show meaning, analyzing word parts, and semantic mapping. | |
| **7. Metacognitive Strategies** | *Metacognition* is defined as awareness and understanding of one's own thought processes. It means "thinking about one's thinking" after learning has taken place. For students to be effective learners, they must become aware of how they acquired knowledge, performed tasks, or solved problems (Gagné, Leblanc, & Rousseau, 2009). When students are taught how to self-assess, they become more confident and willing to take on new challenges. Students should continue to ask themselves questions as they work through a learning task: *What do I know? How do I know it? Could I explain this to someone else?* It is also important to build in reflection questions after the learning has occurred. These questions might include *What did I learn? How has my thinking changed? What do I need to learn next?* The strategy of metacognition can be applied across content areas to create self-directed learners. | |
| **8. Class Discussion** | During high-quality formal class discussions, the teacher designs a scenario for students to discuss a specific topic. The teacher becomes the facilitator with prepared, purposeful questions and invites students to speak, ask questions, and justify their thinking. Examples of ways to implement class discussions include think-pair-share, fishbowl, Socratic seminar, and round table. It is helpful to provide students with conversation prompts and set ground rules before beginning this strategy. | |

*(continued)*

**FIGURE 8.5** Surface, Deep, and Transfer Learning—(*continued*)

| Strategy | Explanation | Surface? Deep? Transfer? |
|---|---|---|
| **9. Peer Tutoring** | Peer tutoring is a teaching strategy that pairs students together to work on academic content or various skills, such as critical thinking, problem solving, and social and emotional behaviors. This strategy has been shown to improve student relationships and academic achievement. Peer tutoring benefits tutors because they learn to become leaders, improve communication skills, and gain a deeper understanding of content as they teach their peers. Tutored students benefit from the relationship because they hone their knowledge and skills, gain confidence, form peer relationships, and improve communication. | |
| **10. Problem-Solving Teaching** | Problem-solving teaching is a teaching strategy that presents students with real-world problems within the context of a subject area requiring investigation, critical thinking, and collaboration to solve. When students are provided with high-interest, relevant topics, they feel more motivated and develop necessary skills for adapting to our ever-changing world. Students should not know the problem in advance but apply prior knowledge and skills to achieve the goal. Planning is key to success. Teachers should plan and teach the content skills needed for the lesson ahead of the investigation, model problem-solving strategies, use success criteria, and give plenty of time for the task. | |
| **11. Identifying Underlying Similarities and Differences** | The strategy of identifying similarities and differences is key to helping learners make connections to prior knowledge, compare information, and categorize concepts. Identifying similarities and differences helps learners gain insight, make inferences and generalizations, and develop or refine schemas (Holyoak & Morrison, 2005). There is a variety of ways to develop this strategy in the classroom. Using compare-and-contrast strategies—such as categorizing objects and ideas to look for connections and using | |

| Strategy | Explanation | Surface? Deep? Transfer? |
|---|---|---|
| **11. Identifying Underlying Similarities and Differences —(continued)** | metaphors to highlight similarities and analogies for differences—helps students to think critically and process new information. Cognitive research indicates that educational programs should challenge students to link, connect, and integrate ideas (Bransford, Brown, & Cocking, 1999). | |
| **12. Imagery** | Imagery is a strategy that helps learners construct mental images as they read or hear information. To help students understand new concepts, teachers may use visual images that lead them to make connections and get a clear picture of the idea. Good readers must learn to construct mental pictures as they read. Through guided visualization, students learn how to connect prior knowledge to the author's writing. | |
| **13. Concept Mapping** | Concept maps are visual organizations and representations of knowledge and information. They are powerful because they help students chunk information based on meaningful connections. Concept maps allow learners to uncover the big-picture idea by starting with higher-level concepts and connecting the details. The visual elements are a powerful way to help the learner see the relationships between different topics, analyze information, and make comparisons. Concept maps are more meaningful when the learner creates them. Some examples of concept maps include spider maps, flowcharts, hierarchy/ chronological maps, and system maps. | |
| **14. Transforming Conceptual Knowledge** | For students to become successful learners, they need to move from learning isolated facts and skills to using problem-solving strategies that they can transfer from one context to another. These skills will enable them to navigate many types of situations they encounter throughout their lives. Educators must design lessons that help students see big-picture ideas, recognize patterns, and | |

*(continued)*

**FIGURE 8.5**    Surface, Deep, and Transfer Learning—(*continued*)

| Strategy | Explanation | Surface? Deep? Transfer? |
|---|---|---|
| **14. Transforming Conceptual Knowledge—** (*continued*) | make generalizations. Learning activities that ask students to move from the factual level to the conceptual level will aid them in transferring ideas across content areas. Educators should provide opportunities for learners to move along the progression from sorting and classifying information to making connections (applying knowledge) among ideas to, finally, transferring concepts in the form of debates, simulations, and case studies. | |
| **15. Self-Regulation** | Self-regulated learning is a cyclical process that consists of motivation, planning, monitoring, and evaluation. Through metacognition, students reflect on and adjust their learning before moving on to the next task. Learners who can plan, set goals, choose strategies, monitor themselves, and reflect tend to be self-motivated and less stressed. Teachers must explicitly model the process of self-regulation and give students multiple opportunities to practice this strategy. Research shows that there is a correlation between using self-regulation strategies and achieving higher academic performance levels. | |
| **16. Note Taking** | Note taking is the process of recording key information from different sources or platforms, such as lectures, field trips, flipped classrooms, videos, and interviews. Note taking is a powerful cognitive tool that actively engages the brain to connect to and retain information. Adding images to represent words or concepts during the note-taking process has a positive effect on memory and understanding of information. When students are able to take notes for themselves, their engagement in learning increases and they develop a stronger sense of self-efficacy. | |

| Strategy | Explanation | Surface? Deep? Transfer? |
|---|---|---|
| **17. Reciprocal Teaching** | Reciprocal teaching is a strategy used across content areas to bolster students' reading comprehension and understanding of a given topic. When teachers and students use this strategy, they share in the teaching and discussion through a structured dialogue. The teacher begins by modeling the four steps: summarizing, questioning, clarifying, and predicting. Then students work in small groups where they take turns assuming the lead role of the teacher to walk their group through the four-step process dialoguing about the reading assignment. Reciprocal teaching actively engages students in the learning process, teaches them to ask meaningful questions, and makes the text more comprehensible. | |

Hint: check out the Key Takeaways for this chapter (p. 124) to learn more about this activity.

### Transfer Learning: Applying Understanding

Hattie (2012) defines *transfer learning* as "the process of developing sufficient surface knowledge to then move to deeper understanding such that one can appropriately transfer this learning to new tasks and situations." Returning to our example of learning to play a musical instrument, students who have learned to sight-read and perform music can apply that knowledge to learn how to play a different instrument. Of course, it takes time to learn to play any instrument, but a student who has already learned to play one instrument would certainly learn more quickly than a student with no musical ability at all. Transfer learning can also be considered as a way to demonstrate a grasp of more advanced skills or concepts by extending prior knowledge while understanding how to apply learning "from one situation to a new situation" (Hattie, 2016).

## Success Criteria: Step 4

After teams have selected instructional strategies, they can refer to the success criteria for Step 4, as shown in Figure 8.6.

The Leader's Role in Step 4

As a leader, your role in Step 4 is to support teachers in creating optimal learning environments. You can do this by providing release time so teachers can model highly effective instructional strategies for other team members. Or you can use classroom walkthroughs to support the implementation of learning progressions, success criteria, and high-impact instructional strategies. See if the learning target is visible to students, and ask them about their success criteria.

**FIGURE 8.6**  Success Criteria: Step 4

| ✓ | Strategies directly target the strengths and gaps identified during Step 3: Create baseline evidence statements. |
| --- | --- |
| ✓ | Teams describe and choose research-based strategies (for each performance group, if possible). |
| ✓ | Teachers prioritize high-impact strategies to use between pre- and post-assessments. |
| ✓ | Strategies selected will improve teachers' instructional delivery and practice. |
| ✓ | Teams agree that strategies selected are high-yield and high-impact. |

## Key Takeaways

- Step 4 teams select high-impact strategies targeted to student needs.
- These strategies are based on the evidence statement created in Step 3, and their intent is to advance student learning.
- Teams and teachers choose strategies and evaluate which ones worked best during the continuous cycle of Achievement Teams.
- Answers to the activity in Figure 8.5 are as follows: 1. D, 2. T, 3. S, 4. S, 5. S, 6. S, 7. D, 8. D, 9. T, 10. T, 11. T, 12. D, 13. D, 14. T, 15. D, 16. S, 17. D.

# 9

# Achievement Teams in Action

*Never be afraid to try something new. Remember:*
*An amateur built the Ark—professionals built the Titanic.*

—Unknown

After teachers and leaders start Achievement Teams, one question always remains: How many pre- and post-cycles should we conduct in a single school year? Our response is simple: as often as teams are willing to evaluate the effects of their teaching. To give you an example, one middle school we worked with committed tentatively to a minimum of six cycles per instructional year.

Clearly, a single cycle will not lend itself to continuous improvement. Achievement Teams are formative; the more opportunities there are to evaluate assessment results and instruction, the greater the likelihood that teaching and learning will improve. Moreover, we cannot increase levels of collective teacher efficacy if we decide that collaboration is a waste of time or that "I work better on my own." We maximize collective efficacy by sharing master and vicarious experiences. As Mike Schmoker (1999) notes, "collaboration allows teachers to capture each other's fund of collective intelligence" (p. 100). The more we collaborate, the more we learn from one another.

In some cases, teams may hyper-analyze mountains of assessment results without collaborating around the *cause* of those effects. Achievement Teams focus on cause rather than just effect and thus have the opportunity to improve instruction. This is especially true when it comes to solving gaps in achievement. Because team members explore all the many reasons that may have caused a problem before determining a solution, teams become more adept at addressing a problem in its entirety.

We have discovered that we can actualize school improvement through the Achievement Teams framework. We use our assessment results to identify specific skills and knowledge that students need to learn well and deeply.

**REFLECTION ACTIVITY**

Opportunities for Growth in Steps 1–4

Now that you and your team members have had an opportunity to review this process, what opportunities for growth might enhance your collaboration and collective efficacy?

| Opportunity for Growth | Action for Improvement | Timeline |
|---|---|---|
| Step 1.<br>Collect and chart the data (formative assessment, pre-/post-assessment). | | |
| Step 2.<br>Set SMART goals. | | |
| Step 3.<br>Create baseline evidence statements. | | |
| Step 4.<br>Select high-yield instructional strategies. | | |

## Implementing and Monitoring the Action Plan

Once your school or district implements Achievement Teams, you need to take steps to properly monitor this initiative. This can include creating a formal feedback system, providing technical support for teaching and learning from facilitators or instructional coaches, and identifying instructional and assessment resources that currently align with Achievement Teams.

As with any new initiative, some changes may take multiple years to accomplish, but others can take place immediately. Action plans help schools and districts start something right away, which is crucial because school systems are more likely to implement changes if they do so within 100 days from the time they adopted those changes.

With guidance from Advanced Collaborative Solutions, a professional development and consulting group, we developed an implementation and action plan for Chalone Peaks Middle School in King City, California, as seen in Figure 9.1. This thoughtful and comprehensive organization of key practices provides a foundation for meaningful action.

Chalone Peaks Middle School planned and monitored six high-impact strategies to support Achievement Teams implementation:

1. Communicate expectations for Achievement Teams.
2. Assemble Achievement Teams.
3. Schedule Achievement Teams leader and administrator meetings.
4. Create an assessment calendar.
5. Create a formalized system for sharing assessment results.
6. Create an internal communication system.

Teachers at the school reported growth between pre- and post-assessment cycles and were able to use feedback to improve performance.

Overall, our team has worked with dozens of districts and hundreds of schools throughout the United States that are implementing Achievement Teams. One school, P.S. 249 in Brooklyn, New York, was recognized with a National Blue Ribbon Award in 2021. Principal Elisa Brown credits much of the school's success to the implementation of Achievement Teams. The school referenced the work in its application for the award:

> One of the most effective models of growth has been collaborative protocols where teachers can learn from colleagues in a safe, growth-focused team setting. Our educators collaborate and learn from one another

**FIGURE 9.1**  Action Plan for Chalone Peaks Middle School

| Present Reality | Our Action Plan (Strategy) | Date to Be Completed | Person Responsible | Expected Results |
|---|---|---|---|---|
| **Communicate expectations for Achievement Teams.** | • Increase collective efficacy among teachers.<br>• Commit to a pre-/post-assessment schedule.<br>• Work together with all staff to ensure fidelity of the process.<br>• Motivate students to exert extra effort by being a part of the process.<br>• Increase levels of student success. | Winter 2019 | All certified trainers, administration, faculty, and the students | • Evidence will show that teachers appropriate new knowledge and sensitively challenge current thinking and practice.<br>• Collaboration time will look and sound different.<br>• Collaboration time is protected.<br>• Teams follow protocol consistently. |
| **Assemble Achievement Teams.** | • Current consensus is to form teams that promote cross-curricular focus (ELA, history, and science), with a subgroup for mathematics.<br>• Teams meet by grade level. | Fall 2019 | Administration, all faculty, and certified trainers | • There is a deeper focus on articulation among content areas.<br>• Schoolwide delivery model is consistent and purposeful.<br>• There are intentional levels of schoolwide implementation.<br>• Students understand the purpose of assessment and reflection. |

| Task | Details | Timeline | Responsible | Rationale |
|---|---|---|---|---|
| **Schedule Achievement Teams leader and administrator meetings.** | • Suggested debrief sessions may occur within a week of the pre-assessment and within a week after the post-assessment. • Meetings may occur in person or electronically via minutes template. | **2019** September October December **2020** January February March April | Achievement Team Certified Trainers and administration | • Meetings between facilitators and leaders increase levels of communication. • Meetings can be used to resolve achievement issues, protocol issues, and overall implementation. • Celebration is key to consistent implementation—take time to share good news. |
| **Create assessment calendar.** | • Teams tentatively commit to a minimum of six cycles per instructional year. • A cycle is the administration of a pre-/post-assessment. | Summer 2019 | Instructional staff and administration content representation by grade level | • A coordinated school assessment calendar gives students multiple opportunities to demonstrate proficiency. • There is a consistent window of the administration of both pre- and post-assessments. |
| **Create formalized system for posting/sharing Achievement Team charts and graphs.** | • Results between pre- and post-assessment must be shared with individual students. • Students will notice that goal setting is a priority throughout the school. • Data walls and data halls do not shame students. | 2019–2020 school year | Instructional staff, with monitoring/feedback from administration | • Goal setting has the potential to double student progress. • Goal setting helps students self-assess their own progress. • Goal setting helps students exert extra effort between pre- and post-assessments. |
| **Create internal communication system.** | Sample Achievement Team Newsletter: http://www.steveventura.com//files/at_feeedback.pdf | Ongoing throughout school year | Administration | • Regular communication/monitoring of Achievement Teams helps keep teams motivated and focused. |

through the Achievement Teams model. Here they meet regularly to review student data, make instructional decisions, and review their performance as educators, all with the common goal of increasing student achievement. Overall, we know that these high expectations coupled with our focus on professional learning have allowed us to achieve great things as a school community. (National Blue Ribbon Schools, 2021, para. 3)

We can lose our ability to focus if we have too many priorities (Reeves & Hattie, 2011). These six strategies provide a strong foundation for deeper and more consistent implementation. One big mistake that people make in leading change is not creating a sense of necessity (Besser & McNulty, 2011). An Achievement Teams action plan does just that; it can empower stakeholders with a sense of conviction because the scope of the work really matters. Schools can use their plan to share a powerful vision and develop a clear path to attain that vision.

## Action Plan Key Points

As teams discover the tactical elements that will have the greatest effect on student achievement, remember to

1. Specify all actions needed to address high-impact strategies.
2. Ensure that all stakeholders have access to the Achievement Teams action plan.
3. Develop explicit plans for each major high-impact strategy.
4. Identify what you will measure and monitor.
5. Update and maintain your plan.

## How Do You Know When Teams Are Successful?

Often, leaders ask us to provide insight into how we measure success with Achievement Teams. Although there is no one way to measure success, it's important to ascertain if your teams are collaborative, if they're making decisions to improve teaching and learning, and if they are seeing results in student outcomes.

We developed the Achievement Teams survey in Figure 9.2 to help teams understand if they are working effectively as a group. Leaders and teams can use the rubric in Figure 9.3, based on a structure developed by Roger Sapsford (1999), to analyze teams' success, identify concerns, and celebrate successes.

**FIGURE 9.2**  Achievement Teams Survey

**Directions:** Please indicate your level of agreement with each of the following statements about your team and school. When the questions ask details about your team, please answer based upon the team that you primarily work with. The answers range from strongly disagree (SD) to strongly agree (SA). You can access this survey online at www.steveventura.com/achievement-teams/resources-from-the-book.php or via the QR code on this page.

(Strongly Disagree) (Disagree) (Neither Agree nor Disagree) (Agree) (Strongly Agree)

| | | | | | |
|---|---|---|---|---|---|
| 1. The purpose of our collaboration is to assess where we are and then prioritize where we need to be by analyzing student assessment results. | SD | D | N | A | SA |
| 2. The members of my team actively participate in and attend all meetings. | SD | D | N | A | SA |
| 3. Our team builds relational trust so collaboration can occur under the most positive conditions. | SD | D | N | A | SA |
| 4. Team members select instructional strategies that have the greatest potential to improve student achievement. | SD | D | N | A | SA |
| 5. The process of goal setting between pre- and post-assessment is a regular practice of our team. | SD | D | N | A | SA |
| 6. The decisions our team makes about instructional practices consist of team dialogue and purposeful facilitation. | SD | D | N | A | SA |
| 7. Every team member enters assessment results into the Achievement Teams data collection template prior to the meeting. | SD | D | N | A | SA |
| 8. As a team, we agree to discontinue ineffective instructional strategies and invest in pedagogically sound practice. | SD | D | N | A | SA |
| 9. Our team follows the Achievement Teams four-step protocol consistently. | SD | D | N | A | SA |
| 10. At the end of our meeting, team members know what learning actions to take before the next meeting. | SD | D | N | A | SA |
| 11. Our team believes the data we collect is an assessment of our instruction and not just used to grade students. | SD | D | N | A | SA |
| 12. Our team dialogue is focused on examining assessment results related to performance and the attainment of goals. | SD | D | N | A | SA |
| 13. When our team meets, all intended actions are recorded based on thoughtful dialogue. | SD | D | N | A | SA |

**FIGURE 9.3**   Achievement Teams Survey Rubric for Analysis and Interpretation

| Collaborative Dialogue Questions | 6, 12, 13 |
|---|---|
| Action Planning Questions | 4, 8, 11 |
| Results in Action Questions | 1, 2, 3, 5, 7, 9, 10 |

| Degree of Collaboration | Collaborative Dialogue | Action Planning | Results in Action |
|---|---|---|---|
| 4–5 | Meeting dialogue opportunities are pre-planned, prioritized, and documented. Team members are fully engaged in collaborative conversations during Achievement Teams sessions. Teams use dialogue to examine assessment results, make sound instructional decisions, and analyze the group's impact on student outcomes. Group members have a shared purpose and collaborate to achieve essential outcomes. | All actions are informed by group conversation. The process for making decisions is clear to all participants. Group leaders are purposefully selected by school leadership and both active and visible within the team. Team members consistently make decisions about what actions they will initiate, change, and stop based on collaborative discussion and assessment review that occur during meetings. Decisions are directly related to teacher practice and student outcomes. | Team members consistently take specific actions as a result of group decisions. Member actions are meaningful and are directly related to teacher practice and student outcomes. |
| 2–3 | Meeting dialogue opportunities exist. Most team members regularly meet. Process for dialogue tends to be improvised or unplanned, but the focus is usually related to making sound instructional | Decisions are usually informed by group conversation. The team's decision-making process might be unclear to many group members. A team leader exists but is not fulfilling the role of facilitator. The team | Team members may take specific actions but not always as a result of group decisions. Group actions might be coordinated and interdependent of other team members or actions. Some actions may |

| Degree of Collaboration | Collaborative Dialogue | Action Planning | Results in Action |
|---|---|---|---|
| 2–3 (continued) | decisions and analyzing the group's impact on student outcomes. Group will occasionally discuss a shared purpose. Professional tension tends to go unrecognized or unresolved. | occasionally makes decisions about what practices they will initiate, change, and stop. Decisions are generally related to teacher practice and student outcomes. | lack complexity or deeper challenge, but are generally related to the teacher practice and student outcomes. |
| 0–1 | Team meeting attendance is low, or the group meets sporadically. Agendas are unplanned or crafted at the last minute. Any dialogue process is improvised. Disagreements do not exist or are unrecognized. Team members may be uninterested or confused. Team members may discuss frustrations privately after the meetings. | A decision-making process is not clear to team members or does not exist. Decisions are rarely agreed upon via group dialogue. Group leaders are not purposefully chosen, do not exist, or may not be visible. Most decisions are unrelated to teacher practice and student outcomes. | Team members take minimal action. Group actions tend to be uncoordinated and unplanned and lack challenge. Actions are typically unrelated to teacher practice and student outcomes. |

# The 10-Day Challenge

Figure 9.4 shows a 10-day challenge (available as a poster at www.steveventura. com/achievement-teams/resources-from-the-book.php or via the QR code on this page) we developed to enable teams to find a short-term win. The purpose of this challenge is to dive in and get the process started, not to worry about perfection. The 10 days don't need to be consecutive; the challenge is meant to take about two weeks. Teams can jump-start Achievement Teams in one content area, focusing on just one standard.

**FIGURE 9.4**   The Achievement Teams 10-Day Challenge

| | |
|---|---|
| 1. Choose just *one* standard or learning intention that will have a significant impact on student learning. | 6. Analyze the pre-assessment results with your team using the four focus questions on the spreadsheet, and select high-impact instructional strategies. |
| 2. Create a short-cycle assessment based on the "unwrapped" standard and/or alignment with Webb's Depth of Knowledge (DOK). | 7. For one week, teach the critical skills and concepts of that one standard based on students' learning needs. |
| 3. Share/teach students the success criteria of the learning intention/standard. | 8. After one week of instruction, hold a monitoring meeting to determine if the instructional strategies are having a positive effect. |
| 4. Administer the assessment *after* two or three days of instruction (varied, based on teacher judgment) so you can determine the prerequisite skills that students do or don't have. This will be your pre-assessment. | 9. After 10 instructional days, administer the post-assessment (aligned/mirrored with the pre-assessment) and enter the results into the Achievement Teams Google spreadsheet. |
| 5. Enter the results of the pre-assessment in your Achievement Teams Google spreadsheet. | 10. Analyze the post-assessment results with your team using the Achievement Teams reflection template. Identify needs for intervention and/or acceleration. |

 Leading Achievement Teams

When we say *leaders*, we're referring to principals, assistant principals, instructional coaches, lead teachers, department chairs, and central office staff. When leadership is a shared responsibility, it promotes greater buy-in and productivity.

Instructional leadership is a significant factor in facilitating, improving, and promoting students' academic progress. Research studies on school improvement and instructional leader effectiveness have identified dozens of defining characteristics (Hattie, 2009; Robinson, 2011). These include having high expectations of students and teachers, emphasizing instruction, providing professional development, promoting collective teacher efficacy, and using data and feedback to evaluate students' progress. The most contemporary research available (Hattie, 2009; Robinson, 2011) concerning specific leadership behaviors that have the greatest influence on student achievement points to the importance of promoting and participating in teacher learning and development and evaluating leadership impact.

Today's instructional leaders *must* be evaluators. They must routinely assess the effect that they and their colleagues are having on student learning, question what they need to improve, and decide on the evidence they need to do this work. Instructional leaders can create and foster levels of self- and collective efficacy where teachers, instead of being micromanaged or "fixed" by leaders, improve themselves.

American education is at a tipping point; what count most are student success and progress. Complex academic, social, and economic barriers, however, keep many students from meeting their potential. The contemporary challenge for the principal is to break down these barriers and create the conditions for learning. Achievement Teams will enable school leaders to not only establish foundational solutions specific to their school settings, but also take specific, targeted steps to address the needs of the school, its teachers, and, most important, its students.

The sad reality is that schools and districts continue to invest millions of dollars each year purchasing programs designed to increase achievement, only to see these programs wind up in the graveyard of good intentions— the file cabinet. Effective instructional leadership depends less on programs and more on professional practice. As education leaders, we must recognize the difference between the two; for every dollar we invest in teacher and leader competence, we will net a greater gain in student achievement than if we were to spend that money on another program.

## Practice, Not Programs

Three organizational techniques can enhance the implementation of Achievement Teams:

**1. Quick Impact Projects:** Schools can introduce or implement these actions within a single school year. Consider them as steps that will have an immediate impact. Quick wins for Achievement Teams may include

- Creating a list of essential standards.
- Designing deeper levels of teacher clarity through learning progressions and success criteria.
- Implementing a pilot program to introduce all four steps of the Achievement Teams framework.

2. **Challenging Commitments:** These practices may need more planning and professional development, which you can do during session breaks or over the summer. These commitments may include

- Consistently implementing common formative short-cycle assessments based on essential standards.
- Organizing school schedules to permit "sacred" collaboration time to maximize teacher reflection between pre- and post-assessments.
- Incorporating more inclusive methods of instruction and expanding teaching and learning.

3. **Major Tasks:** These actions are usually a combination of Quick Impact Projects and Challenging Commitments. They can take up to two or more years to realize the impact and potential of the entire Achievement Teams initiative. They include

- Ensuring deep, steadfast execution of the Achievement Teams process across all grade levels and departments.
- Incorporating monitoring and feedback tools to solidify schoolwide or district efforts.
- Providing ongoing professional development to ensure the integrity of the Achievement Teams framework.

All these actions we list are foundational practices that require minimum monetary investment. When we commit to and sustain core beliefs and practices, we create a structure for continued success. With determination, focus, and a belief that this work is worth doing, it can become part of the culture of your school and district and will ultimately lead to improved student learning.

# Leadership and the Visible Learning Research

Various leadership practices can increase the speed of progress. Collective teacher efficacy currently sits at the top of the list, with an effect size of 1.34. This means that we can advance learning by up to three years in one instructional year. Hattie uses a color-coded key for rating which instructional strategies (among other factors) have the highest probability of making a difference and which would likely not have the probability to be effective. (You can see the key and the rating of more than 250 influences on student achievement here: https://visible-learning.org/wp-content/uploads/2022/01/250-Influences.pdf.)

When Hattie calculated a 0.36 effect for school leaders, we, like many other leaders, became concerned about an effect that was slightly below the 0.40 average. Like other effects, the 0.36 was an average of all effects associated with instructional leadership. However, several specific practices with effect sizes well above average can potentially accelerate student achievement (Hattie, 2017). These include

- Leaders who see that their major role is to evaluate their own impact (effect size = 0.91).
- Leaders who get everyone in the school working together to know and evaluate their impact (effect size = 0.91).
- Leaders who are explicit with teachers and students about what success looks like (effect size = 0.77).
- Leaders who set appropriate levels of challenge and who never retreat to "just try and do your best" (effect size = 0.57).

In addition, Hattie lists characteristics of strong instructional leaders. They

- Conduct classroom observations.
- Interpret test scores with teachers.
- Focus on instructional issues.
- Ensure a coordinated instructional program.
- Are highly visible.
- Communicate high academic standards.
- Ensure class atmospheres are conducive to learning.

The four leadership profiles listed in the following reflection activity provide a focus for principals and system-level leaders and can be part of a strategic plan for Achievement Teams implementation. Even more obvious is where the focus lands—on you and your people.

## REFLECTION ACTIVITY
### Leadership Profile Checklist

Rate your current leadership profile using the profiles listed below.

| Leadership Profile | Moderate | Approaching | Strong |
| --- | --- | --- | --- |
| Leaders who see that their major role is to evaluate their own impact | | | |
| Leaders who get everyone in the school working together to know and evaluate their impact | | | |
| Leaders who are explicit with teachers and students about what success looks like | | | |
| Leaders who set appropriate levels of challenge and who never retreat to "just try and do your best" | | | |

# Rising to the Occasion

As we wrap up this journey, we have to recognize that increasing student achievement involves much more than just following a four-step process. Our intent for creating Achievement Teams was never to overly hype data analysis and assessment without considering the components of human capital, like loyalty, health, and happiness.

One of our favorite books about creating a culture that can raise educational outcomes and productivity is *The Happiness Advantage* (2010), by Shawn Achor. The premise is simple: happiness produces success. It reminds us that schools and the practices we implement have the potential to create long-lasting habits of praise and social support. We know that positive or negative coworkers can affect our happiness and health; as leaders, we can make positive changes to our mindsets, causing others to experience that positivity. Leaders can also encourage effective collaboration by communicating affirmation and the need to be present, not distracted.

In fact, we praise the process of collaboration and Achievement Teams rather than just the outcomes because we're increasing the level of social exchanges that promote shared accountability. Some of the best principals we have worked with not only monitor Achievement Teams implementation, but also are skilled practitioners who provide clarity and accurate feedback.

## Implementation Is Free

Because of their potential to hold schools and teams together, regardless of challenging times, Achievement Teams can improve school culture by infusing the power of collective efficacy. It doesn't cost anything to collaborate, especially when that collaboration focuses on student achievement.

Attitudes play an important role when implementing new initiatives, and high levels of optimism coupled with gratitude can go a long way toward forming a schoolwide community. In 2006, researchers Greenberg and Arakawa discovered that managers who provided frequent recognition and encouragement saw an increase in productivity of 31 percent. Opportunities abound to lead and change culture.

For readers of this book, our hopes are simple. We hope you

1. Understand the content of this book so you can share it with your colleagues.
2. Realize that collaboration should be focused, strong, and interdependent.
3. Value one another every day as team members. Simply put, educators who are valued will stay motivated.

Remember, teachers can't focus on everything. We can use Achievement Teams to identify specific skills and knowledge that students need to learn well and deeply. As they support this process, school leaders can help teachers think about what they can stop doing so they can start focusing on instructional practices that truly make a difference.

# References

Absolum, M. (2011). *Clarity in the classroom*. Portage & Main Press.

Achor, S. (2010). *The happiness advantage: The seven principles of positive psychology that fuel success and performance at work*. Crown Business.

Advanced Collaborative Solutions. (2020). *Achievement Teams instructional strategy flip book*. Author. https://www.steveventura.com/files/di.pdf

Ainsworth, L. (2003). *Power standards: Identifying the standards that matter most*. Advanced Learning Press.

Ainsworth, L. (2010). *Rigorous curriculum design*. Lead and Learn Press.

Ainsworth, L. (2015). *Common formative assessments 2.0*. Corwin.

Bandura, A. (1986). *Social foundations of thought and action: A social cognitive theory*. Prentice Hall.

Bandura, A. (1997). *Self-efficacy: The exercise of control*. W. H. Freeman.

Bandura, A. (2000). Exercise of human agency through collective efficacy. *Current Directions in Psychological Science, 9*, 75–78.

Besser, L., & McNulty, B. (2011). *Leaders make it happen*. Lead and Learn Press.

Biggs, J. B., & Collis, K. F. (1982). *Evaluating the quality of learning: The SOLO taxonomy*. Academic Press.

Blanchard, K. (2015). *How we lead: Conversations with Ken Blanchard*. www.howwelead.org

Bransford, J. D., Brown, A. L., & Cocking, R. R. (Eds.). (1999). *How people learn: Brain, mind, experience, and school*. National Academy Press.

Bryk, S., & Schneider, B. (2002). *Trust in schools: A core resource for improvement*. Russell Sage Foundation.

Comaford, C. (2013). *Smart tribes: How teams become brilliant together*. Portfolio.

Doran, G. T. (1981). There's a S.M.A.R.T way to write management's goals and objectives. *Management Review (AMA Forum), 70*(11), 35–36.

Doyle, A. C. (1891). *A scandal in Bohemia*. Newnes.

DuFour, R., & Fullan, M. (2013). *Cultures built to last: Systemic PLCs at work*. Solution Tree.

Elmore, R. F., City, E. A., Fiarman, S. E., & Teitel, L. (2009). *Instructional rounds in education: A network approach to improving teaching and learning*. Harvard Education Publishing Group.

Fendick, F. (1990). *The correlation between teacher clarity of communication and student achievement gain: A meta-analysis*. Unpublished doctoral dissertation, University of Florida.

Fisher, D., Frey, N., & Hattie, J. (2016). *Visible learning for literacy: Implementing the practices that work best to accelerate student learning*. Corwin.

Futernick, K. (2007). *A possible dream: Retaining California teachers so all students learn*. California State University.

Gagné, P., Leblanc, N., & Rousseau, A. (2009). *Apprendre... une question de stratégies: Développer les habiletés liées aux fonctions exécutives*. Les Éditions de la Chenelière.

Gino, F. (2019). Cracking the code of sustained collaboration: Six new tools for training people to work together better. *Harvard Business Review, 97*(6), 72–81.

Goddard, R. D., Hoy, W. K., & Hoy, A. W. (2000). Collective teacher efficacy: Its meaning, measure, and effect on student achievement. *American Education Research Journal, 37*(2), 479–502.

Greenberg, M. H., & Arakawa, D. (2006, October 10). *Optimistic managers and their influence on productivity and employee engagement.* University of Pennsylvania. https://repository.upenn.edu/cgi/viewcontent.cgi?article=1003&context=mapp_capstone

Guarino, C. M., Santibañez, L., & Daley, G. A. (2006). Teacher recruitment and retention: A review of the recent empirical literature. *Review of Educational Research, 76*(2), 173–208.

Hake, R. (1998). Interactive-engagement versus traditional methods: A six-thousand-student survey of mechanics test data for introductory physics courses. *American Journal of Physics, 66*(1), 64–74.

Haladyna, T. M. (2012). *Developing and validating multiple-choice test items* (3rd ed.). Routledge.

Hattie, J. (2009). *Visible learning: A synthesis of over 800 meta-analyses relating to achievement.* Routledge.

Hattie, J. (2012). *Visible learning for teachers: Maximizing impact on learning.* Routledge.

Hattie, J. (2017). Don't be a hero. *Leader.* http://www.leadermagazine.co.uk/articles/dont_be_a_hero/

Hattie, J. A. C., & Donoghue, G. M. (2016, August 10). Learning strategies: A synthesis and conceptual model. *npj Science of Learning, 1*(16013).

Hattie, J., & Hamilton, A. (2020). *Real gold vs. fool's gold: The Visible Learning methodology for finding what works best in education.* Corwin & Cognition Education Group. www.visible-learning.com/sites/default/files/Real%20Gold%20vs.%20Fools%20Gold_FINAL_app.pdf

Hattie, J., & Timperley, H. (2007). The power of feedback. *Review of Educational Research, 77*(1), 81–112.

Hattie, J., & Zierer, K. (2018). *10 mindframes for visible learning: Teaching for success.* Routledge.

Heck, R. H., Marcoulides, G. A., & Lang, P. (1991). Principal instructional leadership and school achievement: The application of discriminant techniques. *School Effectiveness and School Improvement, 2*(2), 115–135.

Heflebower, T., Hoegh, J. K., & Warrick, P. B. (2014). *A school leader's guide to standards-based grading.* Marzano Resources.

Heflebower, T., Hoegh, J. K., Warrick, P. B., & Flygare, J. (2019). *A teacher's guide to standards-based learning.* Marzano Resources.

Heritage, M. (2008). *Learning progressions: Supporting instruction and formative assessment.* National Center for Research on Evaluation, Standards, and Student Testing (CRESST).

Heritage, M. (2010). *Formative assessment: Making it happen in the classroom.* Corwin.

Heritage, M. (2011, Spring). Formative assessment: An enabler of learners. *Better: Evidence-Based Education, 3*(3).

Holyoak, K. J., & Morrison, R. G. (Eds.). (2005). *The Cambridge handbook of thinking and reasoning.* Cambridge University Press.

Ishikawa, K. (1989). *Introduction to quality control.* Springer.

Knight, J. (2012). *High-impact instruction: A framework for great teaching.* Corwin.

Knight, J. (2014). *Focus on teaching: Using video for high-impact instruction.* Corwin.

Knight, J. (2019). Why teacher autonomy is central to coaching success. *Educational Leadership, 77*(3). www.ascd.org/publications/educational-leadership/nov19/vol77/num03/Why-Teacher-Autonomy-Is-Central-to-Coaching-Success.aspx

Madden, L. E. (1997). Motivating students to learn better through own goal-setting. *Education, 117*(3), 411–415.

Marzano, R. J. (2011). The art and science of teaching: Making the most of instructional rounds. *Educational Leadership, 68*(5), 80–81.

Mertler, C. A. (2001). Designing scoring rubrics for your classroom. *Practical Assessment, Research, and Evaluation, 7*(25). https://scholarworks.umass.edu/cgi/viewcontent.cgi?article=1108&context=pare

Miller, G. A. (1956). The magical number seven, plus or minus two: Some limits on our capacity for processing information. *Psychological Review, 63*(2), 81–97.

National Blue Ribbon Schools. (2021). PS 249—The Caton School—Brooklyn, NY. https://nationalblueribbonschools.ed.gov/awardwinners/winning/21ny115pu_ps_249_caton_the.html

National Reading Panel. (2000). *Teaching children to read: An evidence-based assessment of the scientific research literature on reading and its implications for reading instruction* (NIH Publication No. 00-4769). National Institute of Child Health and Human Development, National Institutes of Health.

Nichols, P. (2010). What is a learning progression? *Pearson: Test, Measure, and Research Services Bulletin, Issue 12.* http://images.pearsonassessments.com/images/tmrs/tmrs_rg/Bulletin_12.pdf?WT.mc_id=TMRS_Bulletin_12_What_is_a_learning_progression

Nitko, A. J. (2001). *Educational assessment of students* (3rd ed.). Merrill.

Popham, W. J. (2003). The seductive allure of data. *Educational Leadership, 60*(5), 48–51. https://www.ascd.org/el/articles/the-seductive-allure-of-data

Popham, W. J. (2008). *Transformative assessment.* ASCD.

Reeves, D. (2010). *Finding your leadership focus: What matters most for student results.* Teachers College Press.

Reeves, D. B., & Hattie, J. (2011). *Activate: A leader's guide to people, practices, and processes.* Lead and Learn Press.

Robinson, V. (2011). *Student-centered leadership.* Jossey-Bass.

Sapsford, R. (1999). *Survey research.* SAGE.

Schmoker, M. (1999). *Results: The key to continuous school improvement* (2nd ed.). ASCD.

Schunk, D. H. (1985). Participation in goal setting: Effects on self-efficacy and skills of learning-disabled children. *Journal of Special Education, 19*, 307–317.

SNFQAPI. (2019). *Quality assurance & performance improvement.* https://www.snfqapi.com/resources/root-cause-analysis

Stake, R. (2004). *Standards-based and responsive evaluation.* SAGE.

Venables, D. R. (2011). *The practice of authentic PLCs: A guide to effective teacher teams.* Corwin.

Wammes, J. D., Meade, M. E., & Fernandes, M. A. (2016). The drawing effect: Evidence for reliable and robust memory benefits in free recall. *Quarterly Journal of Experimental Psychology, 69*(9).

Webb, N. (1997). *Research monograph number 6: Criteria for alignment of expectations and assessments on mathematics and science education.* Council of Chief State School Officers.

Wiggins, G. (2012). Seven keys to effective feedback. *Educational Leadership, 70*(1), 10–16.

# Index

# About the Authors

 **Steve Ventura** is the president and lead consultant at Advanced Collaborative Solutions. He is a highly motivational and knowledgeable speaker who approaches high-stakes professional development armed with practical, research-based strategies. Steve is a former elementary and secondary teacher and has worked as both a school and a district-level administrator. He has published multiple books and articles and regularly presents and keynotes at global education events. He is passionate about helping school-based leaders instill a culture grounded in collective teacher efficacy through his flagship work, Achievement Teams. Through this collaborative work, Steve has helped countless educators improve their teaching practice.

 **Michelle Ventura** is cofounder of and a professional learning consultant with Advanced Collaborative Solutions. With 30 years of classroom experience, she brings a unique and sensible perspective to professional development grounded in effective teaching and learning. Michelle is passionate about the teaching profession and firmly believes that all kids can learn. She is known for creating engaging adult learning opportunities that provide participants with immediate possibilities to improve teacher practice. Most days, she can be found leading educators through sessions on Achievement Teams and high-impact instructional strategies.

## Related ASCD Resources: Instructional Leadership and Teacher Teams

At the time of publication, the following resources were available (ASCD stock numbers appear in parentheses).

### Print Products

*The Artisan Teaching Model for Instructional Leadership: Working Together to Transform Your School* by Kenneth Baum and David Krulwich (#116041)

*C.R.A.F.T. Conversations for Teacher Growth: How to Build Bridges and Cultivate Expertise* by Sally J. Zepeda, Lakesha Robinson Goff, and Stefanie W. Steele (#120001)

*Creating a Culture of Reflective Practice: Capacity-Building for Schoolwide Success* by Pete Hall and Alisa Simeral (#117006)

*The Definitive Guide to Instructional Coaching: Seven Factors for Success* by Jim Knight (#121006)

*The eCoaching Continuum for Educators: Using Technology to Enrich Professional Development and Improve Student Outcomes* by Marcia Rock (#117048)

*Educational Coaching: A Partnership for Problem Solving* by Cathy A. Toll (#118027)

*Facilitating Teacher Teams and Authentic PLCs: The Human Side of Leading People, Protocols, and Practices* by Daniel R. Venables (#117004)

*The Instructional Playbook: The Missing Link for Translating Research into Practice* by Jim Knight, Ann Hoffman, Michelle Harris, and Sharon Thomas (#122020)

*Intentional and Targeted Teaching: A Framework for Teacher Growth and Leadership* by Douglas Fisher, Nancy Frey, and Stefani Arzonetti Hite (#116008)

*The PD Curator: How to Design Peer-to-Peer Professional Learning That Elevates Teachers and Teaching* by Lauren Porosoff (#121029)

*Peer Coaching to Enrich Professional Practice, School Culture, and Student Learning* by Pam Robbins (#115014)

*Uprooting Instructional Inequity: The Power of Inquiry-Based Professional Learning* by Jill Harrison Berg (#121016)

For up-to-date information about ASCD resources, go to **www.ascd.org**. You can search the complete archives of *Educational Leadership* at **www.ascd.org/el**.

### ASCD myTeachSource®

Download resources from a professional learning platform with hundreds of research-based best practices and tools for your classroom at http://myteachsource.ascd.org/.

For more information, send an email to member@ascd.org; call 1-800-933-2723 or 703-578-9600; send a fax to 703-575-5400; or write to Information Services, ASCD, 2800 Shirlington Road, Suite 1001, Arlington, VA 22206 USA.

# THE WHOLE CHILD

The ASCD Whole Child approach is an effort to transition from a focus on narrowly defined academic achievement to one that promotes the long-term development and success of all children. Through this approach, ASCD supports educators, families, community members, and policymakers as they move from a vision about educating the whole child to sustainable, collaborative actions.

*Achievement Teams* relates to the **engaged, supported,** and **challenged** tenets. *For more about the ASCD Whole Child approach, visit* **www.ascd.org/wholechild.**

# WHOLE CHILD
# TENETS

**1** **HEALTHY**
Each student enters school healthy and learns about and practices a healthy lifestyle.

**2** **SAFE**
Each student learns in an environment that is physically and emotionally safe for students and adults.

**3** **ENGAGED**
Each student is actively engaged in learning and is connected to the school and broader community.

**4** **SUPPORTED**
Each student has access to personalized learning and is supported by qualified, caring adults.

**5** **CHALLENGED**
Each student is challenged academically and prepared for success in college or further study and for employment and participation in a global environment.